The UNFINISHED EXPERIMENT

DEMOCRACY IN THE DOMINICAN REPUBLIC

The

UNFINISHED

DEMOCRACY IN THE

Juan Bosch

 FREDERICK A. PRAEGER, *Publisher*

EXPERIMENT

DOMINICAN REPUBLIC

New York · Washington · London

FREDERICK A. PRAEGER, PUBLISHERS

111 Fourth Avenue, New York 3, N.Y., U.S.A.

77–79 Charlotte Street, London W.1, England

Published in the United States of America in 1965
by Frederick A. Praeger, Inc., Publishers

First published in Mexico in 1964 under the title
CRISIS DE LA DEMOCRACIA DE AMÉRICA
EN LA REPÚBLICA DOMINICANA
by Centro de Estudios y Documentación Sociales

Library of Congress Catalog Card Number: 65–24937

Printed in the United States of America

To
JOSÉ FRANCISCO PEÑA GÓMEZ,
AND THROUGH HIM,
TO THE YOUTH OF THE PEOPLE,
THE SEED OF HOPE
FOR THE DOMINICAN NATION

Publisher's Note

Writing this book from his exile in Puerto Rico, Juan Bosch observed that the clock of Dominican history, stopped during the Trujillo regime, began to move at double speed once the dictator was dead. After more than thirty years under one government, the Dominican Republic has seen more than a half-dozen regimes come and go in the past four years. The only one of these to come to power through a popular election was Dr. Bosch's, inaugurated in February, 1963. With the victory of Dr. Bosch and his party—the PRD—the Dominican Republic was hailed as a "showcase of democracy," as proof that the disease of dictatorship was not chronic and that a healthy democracy could be established within the body politic. But seven months after he took office, Dr. Bosch was sent into exile, the victim of a military coup.

During his enforced retirement, Dr. Bosch wrote this book assessing the course of his country's history from Trujillo's assassination, in May, 1961, to May, 1964, another time of rebellion. But the inconclusive events of May, 1964, with which Dr. Bosch ends his book, were merely a prelude to the bloody eruption in April of 1965.

The clock of history, as Dr. Bosch predicted, now moved faster.

The most recent ordeal of the Dominican people lies beyond the scope of this volume, but theirs is a country where "The Dead Still Live"—as Dr. Bosch titled a story he wrote twenty years ago, during an earlier exile. When he returned to his native land in October of 1961, he realized that Trujillo's ghost had not been laid, and he continues to fight Trujillo's legacy today, as he did during his term in office.

Much of Trujillo's spirit survives among the leaders of the Armed Forces, who tend to consider themselves as the sole guardians of the state, and the military *caudillo* is a frequent figure in Latin American history. In the Dominican Republic, it was the military who were the prime movers in the overthrow of the Bosch government in 1963 —accusing it of being soft on Communism and generally ineffective. During the ensuing period, it seemed clear that if governmental changes were to come, they would have to come from the military or elements of it. Nineteen months passed before pressure built up, but when the outbreak came, it came from younger elements of the military. General Elías Wessin y Wessin now found himself forced to defend the order he had tried to establish, but in the interim, the Dominican Communists had grown markedly stronger, if not in numbers, certainly in political effectiveness.

The widespread discontent that had gathered under the Trujillo dictatorship had broken loose during the intense campaigning of 1962, only to be reined in after the coup against Bosch. This dammed-up political energy was readily tapped by Communist and Communist-front groups. To many, the Communist label itself had become meaningless, since Trujillo had applied it to a variety of enemies of the regime. Even during his presidential campaign, Dr. Bosch had faced—and refuted—this charge many times. But he maintained then, as now, that "Intense fear of Communism creates Communists."

The tragic confusion over the meaning of Communism —and of democracy—which Dr. Bosch and his PRD tried to clarify during the electoral campaign, continued to plague him during his brief tenure in office, and undoubtedly poisoned his relations with some members of the officer corps. Its repercussions extended beyond the President himself to hamstring many of his advisers and even the Alliance for Progress programs. The Communist threat played a role again in April of 1965, when President Johnson, to avoid "another Cuba," ordered the Marines to land in Santo Domingo. Senator J. W. Fulbright and many others have sharply criticized this move. On September 15, 1965, Senator Fulbright commented on the shifts in U.S. policy toward the Dominican Republic:

> In 1963, the United States strongly supported Bosch and the PRD as enlightened reformers; in 1965, the United States opposed their return to power on the unsubstantiated ground that a Bosch or PRD government would certainly, or almost certainly, become Communist-dominated. Thus the United States turned its back on social revolution in Santo Domingo and associated itself with a corrupt and reactionary military oligarchy.

Since not all the reports are in, it is impossible for the Publisher, of course, to evaluate the extent to which Senator Fulbright's charges are justified. No one can say with any certainty what would have happened had President Johnson chosen another course or failed to act, nor can anyone assess how effective the known Communists would have been in Santo Domingo. It is possible that United States intervention thwarted a genuine democratic revolution. It is also possible that United States intervention prevented a Communist take-over. These are things we do not know and perhaps will never know.

Nevertheless, there remain the enduring facts of poverty that kills the will to hope, ignorance that accepts crushing injustice, disease that suffocates the young and ages their parents overnight. Despite the tragic past of the Dominican people, it is not too late to alter these stark truths. If the Dominicans have the will and the strength to establish a government that offers social justice and opportunity for all, there is still time to finish the unfinished experiment. And in this experiment, the United States, from its own experience and resources, can render constructive help to meet the needs of the people directly and immediately.

Preface

This is not a book of memoirs. Therefore, do not expect a narration of the events that a democratic government made possible in the Dominican Republic less than two years after the death of the dictator par excellence, Rafael Leonidas Trujillo, and that precipitated the overthrow of that government by a military coup seven months after it came to power.

This book has been written in order to point out the intrinsic weaknesses of a society that has remained backward because of the organized efforts of forces opposed to its progress. Because of these weaknesses, the democratic government established by the people was also intrinsically weak and unable to withstand its traditional enemies.

A democratic government is sustained by the will of all the social strata and of all the individuals who have responsibilities to it as citizens. If that will is lacking, a democratic government cannot survive. In the Dominican Republic, the most influential strata of the population joined with political leaders, who had gained prestige by fighting tyranny, in a conspiracy to defeat the democratic government. They worked assiduously in the barracks to induce the soldiers to undertake the coup of September 25, 1963. It is lamentable that the soldiers let themselves be led into this adventure, but how could they be expected to act differently when doctors, lawyers, and priests had shown themselves incapable of restraining their passions?

In the Dominican Republic, a noteworthy social phenomenon exists: The masses have greater social consciousness, greater patriotism, and greater awareness of their responsibilities as citizens than the upper and the middle strata of the middle class, which produced the leaders of the 1963 coup. The differences between classes are very apparent. Any unemployed laborer from one of the poor districts in Santo Domingo could give lessons in political honesty to any of the presidential candidates in the 1962 elections. The reasons lie not in the personal virtues of the masses or in the personal vices of the middle classes, but rather in the fact that the former belong to a coherent social group, while the latter do not.

The reader will find in this book a fuller explanation of what has been described above. My deepest hope is that it will be useful and will help him to view Dominican affairs, a very small part of the political events in Latin America, with the perspective I have sought to give. Frequently, social and political happenings in our countries are seen only in relation to outstanding leaders. But the forces behind them—the fingers that manipulate the puppet strings—remain hidden. In a sense, we are all puppets moved by very powerful forces.

Up to a certain point, this book is a continuation of its predecessor, *Trujillo: Causas de una tiranía sin ejemplo* (*Trujillo: Reasons for an Unparalleled Tyranny*), which was written shortly before his death. Trujillo was the product of all the historical forces that have opposed the development of the Dominican people since Columbus discovered the island. Trujillo's dictatorship generated new forces and sustained many old ones. The Dominican people, who will have to combat Trujillo's influence for several years more, did not know that many anti-Trujilloists in reality wanted not to destroy his regime but to substitute themselves at its head. Two years after Trujillo's fall, the coup of September 25, 1963, which overthrew the new democratic government, made this all too clear.

Besides his own sons, Rafael Trujillo left numerous political heirs in the Dominican Republic. The Dominican people will have to purge their land of that bad seed. I have borne my share of this responsibility as a political leader, as a democratic President, and I hope to do so now, as author of this book.

J. B.

Luquillo, Puerto Rico

Contents

The UNFINISHED EXPERIMENT

Death of the Dictator

At midday on May 31, 1961, I was in the dining room of the Institute of Political Education, in San Isidro del Coronado, on the outskirts of San José, Costa Rica. I had finished eating, and was talking with one of the other professors, passing the time until afternoon classes began, when a group of students, led by a Dominican named Llauger Medina, burst in, shouting that Trujillo was dead. A few minutes later, the Honduran Ambassador to Costa Rica telephoned me to confirm the news.

That same afternoon students from the Institute paraded with banners and posters through the streets of San José and organized a rally in Central Park, at which José Figueres, former President of Costa Rica, and I were to speak. At that very time, I was in Figueres' house telephoning Angel Miolán, Secretary General of the Dominican Revolutionary Party (Partido Revolucionario Dominicano, or PRD), who was in Caracas. I asked him to take the first plane to San José, and to summon all available PRD representatives for an urgent meeting in San José. At the time of Trujillo's death, I was President of the party and head of its Political Committee.

Miolán immediately set about telephoning the various sections (the party was organized in sections for each geographic area where there were sufficient members) and then left for Panama, en route to Costa Rica. In Panama, he was told by the air-line office that it had orders not to book passage for Dominicans in the Caribbean area until the situation in Santo Domingo caused by Trujillo's death was cleared up. The Panama–Costa Rica flight was outside the Caribbean zone, and so Miolán succeeded in getting on a plane to San José. But none of the other section delegates was allowed to travel except for two who happened to have U.S. passports—Ramón Castillo, Secretary of the Puerto Rico section, and Nicolás Silfa, Secretary of the New York section.

Consequently, only four PRD leaders assembled in San José—Miolán, Silfa, Castillo, and I. If I remember correctly, it was on June 4 that we began to discuss what would be the outcome of the crisis thrust upon our country by Trujillo's death. From the moment I learned of it, I had felt that the time had come for us to re-enter the Dominican Republic, and as my colleagues arrived, it turned out that each of them had the same idea. All of us believed that now, after more than twenty years of exile, we had an opportunity to lead the Dominican people toward a brighter future, and that we could not afford to miss that opportunity.

But only a few weeks before, on May 19, right in San José, our party had made an agreement with the Dominican Revolutionary Vanguard (Vanguardia Revolucionaria Dominicana, or VRD), to join forces in any action to destroy the Trujillo dictatorship. This understanding obligated us to consult with the Revolutionary Vanguard's leaders before taking any steps. We called the President of the VRD, Horacio Julio Ornes, in San Juan, Puerto Rico, and asked him to meet with us as soon as possible in San José. Ornes could not leave immediately because of the travel ban imposed on Dominicans, and waiting for him made us lose some time. After he finally did arrive, we lost even more time because he said he had to telephone Puerto Rico and consult his associates there. At long last, after several calls to San Juan, he told us that his party did not approve of our plan. The Revolutionary Vanguard leaders believed that returning to the Dominican Republic would constitute a betrayal of the revolution—the thoroughgoing social, economic, and political revolution for which we were all working.

By now, a week had gone by since we had assembled. Finally, on June 13, we sent cables to Joaquín Balaguer, President of the Dominican Republic, and to the head of the Organization of American States mission (which was in Santo Domingo to assist in establishing electoral machinery), saying that if they could provide sufficient guarantees, the Dominican Revolutionary Party would move its leadership to the Dominican Republic. Both answered at once. Balaguer pledged guarantees, and the head of the OAS mission informed us that Balaguer had assured him that the PRD would have guarantees permitting it to function as a political party.

The Trujillo government, left rudderless by the abrupt removal of its leader, had no choice in the matter. In *Trujillo: Reasons for an Unparalleled Tyranny*, written shortly before Trujillo's death, I stated that:

> owing to the fact that Trujillo himself embodied every traditional Dominican shortcoming, and furthermore that his personal temperament was decisive in creating and maintaining the vast enterprise known as the Trujillo regime, that enterprise depends for its existence on Trujillo's personal leadership. This dependence is the weak link in the

tyranny, which cannot last a single day beyond that on which Rafael Leonidas Trujillo loses either his power or his life. The historical circumstances that produced him as a psychological, military, political, and economic being have not been, nor will they ever be, reproduced for his heirs. Not one of them, therefore, will be able to function as he does.*

It was clear to anyone who had seriously studied the characteristics of the Trujillo regime that it could not survive without him. On May 31, at the rally in Central Park in San José, I emphasized that what had happened in Nicaragua would not be repeated in Santo Domingo. In Nicaragua, the death of the dictator Anastasio Somoza had caused no substantial changes in the established order because his sons had continued ruling the country as if nothing had happened. But I felt that Joaquín Balaguer, on the contrary, would find himself in a difficult situation and would have no alternative but to preside over the liquidation of Trujilloism. I had studied the problem of the Dominican social castes for a long time and was convinced that in the struggle for power triggered by Trujillo's death, the so-called first families would inevitably band together. I knew that Balaguer would not join with that group, which he had held himself aloof from all his life and which he did not belong to, either by birth or by inclination. But to avoid exposing himself to attacks by that group, he would immediately have to start dismantling the machinery of the dictatorship.

This reasoning applied to a man playing a key role in the Dominican crisis, but not to the crisis itself. Studying the crisis, apart from the possibly decisive human factors, I concluded that it was caught up in the clash of national and international forces. And at that time, in the middle of June, 1961, international forces were the more powerful.

* Pp. 178–79.

These pressured the entire Dominican regime—not only the civil government headed by Balaguer but also the military led by Rafael ("Ramfis") Trujillo, Jr., the dictator's son—to offer and to enforce the guarantee we requested. If my conclusions were correct—and the facts showed that they were—the Dominican Government would have to yield. It would be forced to give guarantees to the Dominican Revolutionary Party, which, protected by those guarantees, could mobilize the people to win their freedom and carry out a democratic revolution.

Immediately after Trujillo's death, no national movement was forthcoming. Ramfis Trujillo, who was in Europe when his father was shot to death on George Washington Avenue in the Dominican capital, flew to Santo Domingo and took over command of the military. He thereupon devoted his major efforts to satisfying his appetite for revenge and organized a hunt for those who had been a party to the assassination plot. At the same time, he set about getting as many dollars as possible out of the country. Meantime, the nation was paralyzed by an acute economic crisis, caused primarily by the 1957 recession in the United States but aggravated by two other factors: first, Trujillo's excessive spending on sumptuous but unproductive construction projects for the 1955 Peace Fair, and second, the sanctions imposed on the Dominican Republic by the Organization of American States after Trujillo's assassination attempt against Venezuelan President Rómulo Betancourt in June, 1960.

These combined elements had their effect on the Armed Forces, which constituted Ramfis Trujillo's base of power. He needed an international victory to enable him to assure his soldiers that they would retain their positions in the future. The only such triumph he could achieve was the lifting of the OAS sanctions. But how could he get those sanctions lifted while the dictatorship continued? He must give evidence that the regime was going to be liquidated. And what better indication could Ramfis offer than a guarantee of free rein to a democratic party whose leaders were known and respected throughout the Americas.

Still another complication facing the Dominican regime was proving favorable to the PRD. This was the sugar-supply crisis in the United States. The United States had cut itself off from the Dominican sugar market under a resolution prohibiting the purchase of sugar from countries under dictatorial rule. The intention had been to boycott Cuban sugar, but world opinion and even that of an important section of the U.S. public, made it difficult to boycott Cuba and not the Dominican Republic. Fidel Castro had still not declared Cuba a Communist nation, and the Dominican Republic was governed by a dictatorship far older than Castro's. Furthermore, the Organization of American States had denounced the Dominican Government as a violator of international law and imposed sanctions against the country in August, 1960.

The United States, then, was not buying Dominican sugar. But during 1961, U.S. sugar reserves were shrinking, and its sugar-beet crop was not good. Moreover, sugar production threatened to drop in Asia and in Latin American countries free of dictatorship. Thus Washington favored liberalization of the Dominican Government, not only as the solution to a political problem that affected its position in Latin America, but also to pave the way for dropping the boycott on Dominican sugar, an economic move of great importance to U.S. consumers. Ramfis Trujillo and his mother and brothers owned 80 per cent of the Dominican sugar plantations, including the two largest in the world. Moreover, the Trujillo family wanted money even more than power. So when it came to a choice between retaining political power in the Dominican Republic and obtaining dollars by selling sugar to the United States,

Ramfis Trujillo wavered. And we, the PRD leaders, understood the situation and took advantage of his indecision.

Why did we exploit this opportunity? To launch ourselves in the struggle for power?

No. But this simple and emphatic No requires an explanation.

Trujillo's demise had left the country in a state of political agitation, economic distress, and weakened social structure, which necessitated scrupulous political conduct by those who wanted to lead the Dominican people toward a gradual, careful, and bloodless liquidation of the remains of the dictatorship. This could not be achieved without completely changing the Dominican atmosphere. It required, above all, that one ask oneself with utmost honesty, and answer with equal honesty, what one was seeking.

In the struggle for power, two forces could be employed: arms held by the military, and external pressure, which only Washington could apply. To make use of the military, a conspiracy with it would be necessary, and from that conspiracy several generals would emerge with a firm hold on political power. Furthermore, conspiracy was dishonorable, and we had not spent years fighting for our cause only to end up resorting to base and infamous tactics. To enlist Washington would be to renounce the principles that had for long years established our position in the camp of democratic revolution: that the democratic revolution had to be basically national, carried out by forces within the country. As democrats, we could accept aid from democrats in the United States, whether or not they were in power, just as we accepted aid from Latin American democrats. But we could not ally ourselves with any foreign government, no matter how friendly.

Our aim could not be to enter into the struggle for power; rather we must attempt to mobilize the people, and we knew we could not do this in one month or even in six months. We might try to effect the revolution after achieving power, not as a political party but as part of a regime of national unity, but, as will be shown in a later chapter, that was not possible. Therefore, it remained for us to function within the framework of our original intention, that is, of mobilizing the people. In order to accomplish that, we needed nothing but our own efforts.

Mobilizing the people required knowledge of the general mood, an understanding of the psychology of the masses, sector by sector, with an awareness of the exact level that each sector had reached in economic, social, and political evolution. It also required a knowledge of the aspirations of each sector and its capacity to fight. Believing that we knew these things, we laid down a line that must be strictly followed. We would have to arouse both the social and the political consciousness of the people, and simultaneously wipe out the national fear, a fear that lay deep within the people's hearts. To accomplish this, we would direct ourselves first to the great masses, because we believed that they had been less corrupted by the pressures of the dictatorship. Also, this was the group that most needed strong leadership. In our opinion, the middle classes had been corrupted by the destructive forces of Trujilloism and would throw themselves into the struggle for power at the first opportunity.

Our task was not an easy one. To begin with, we lacked the support of the youth in all three strata—upper, middle, and lower—of the middle class. Middle-class youth is the soul of any Latin American political-reform movement. Those of us responsible for charting the course of the Dominican Revolutionary Party had a clear picture of our situation in spite of having been in exile for a quarter of a century. Some of us, Angel Miolán for one, had been in exile even longer. Nevertheless, our appraisal was accurate. The middle-class-youth movement had decided its course before May 30, 1961, and had pursued it until July 5, the historic day on which the PRD arrived in the Dominican Republic. Their movement's course, although these youth expected otherwise, would not be that of the people.

In the last two years of the Trujillo regime, youth of the three middle-class strata had launched an opposition movement against the dictatorship, perhaps stimulated more than anything else by Fidel Castro's successful overthrow of Fulgencio Batista in Cuba. Every middle-class Dominican youngster dreamed of coming down from a mountain to topple Trujillo and then being acclaimed for his feat by the people of the Americas. But the Cuban revolution was not the kind that the Dominican people were capable of supporting. In the middle of 1961, the Dominican masses had no idea what social justice was. They did not know why they were hungry, sick, ignorant, and enslaved. Between the fall of the Cuban dictator Gerardo Machado, in 1933, and the overthrow of Fulgencio Batista in 1958, the Cubans had been exposed to twenty-five years of political education, and all of Cuba supported Fidel in his fight against Batista. But the people of the Dominican Republic had taken no part in the struggle against Trujillo. The middle-class Dominican youth were mostly sons of veteran Trujilloists—lawyers, architects, engineers, businessmen, and plantation owners who had made fortunes because of Trujillo's favors. And in Santo Domingo history gave its eternal answer to political and social conflicts: Sons rebelled against their parents. For many parents, their sons' rebellion against Trujillo—and the imprisonment, torture, and exile that resulted—seemed to absolve them of guilt for continuing to reap the harvest of power until Trujillo's fall.

Around the end of 1959, youths who opposed Trujillo formed a secret political party called the 14th of June Movement (Movimiento 14 de Junio). The name gives an idea of the influence that Fidel Castro's image* had on those young people, but they were by no means Communists. Nor had Castro yet proclaimed himself a Communist. The middle-class Dominican youth admired Fidel as a hero who had overthrown a dictator, as a highly nationalistic leader, but not as the head of a Marxist-Leninist revolution. When the PRD leaders arrived in the Dominican Republic, many of the Catorcita† organizers were in jail, including one of their most prominent members, Dr. Manuel Tavarez Justo, and its meetings were held in secret.

The arrival of the Dominican Revolutionary Party in Santo Domingo on July 5, 1961—thirty-six days after the assassination of Trujillo—gave the people the feeling that they now had leaders who would protect them from tyranny. The bravest young people, men and women from the hunger-belt area of old Santo Domingo de Guzmán, threw themselves into the fight.

This fact is of such importance in Dominican history that it deserves—I would go so far as to say that it demands—a few explanatory paragraphs. Although a number of years have passed, Dominican historians still do not realize the significance of July 5, 1961, as the beginning of the development of a political consciousness in the Dominican masses.

---

* As Castro's movement was originally called the 26th of July Movement, in commemoration of the Cuban revolutionaries' abortive raid on the Moncada barracks in 1953, so June 14, 1959, was the date of the Castro-backed sea-and-air invasion of the Dominican Republic. But in this case, what was to have been a prelude to guerrilla activity was quickly stamped out by Trujillo.—ED.

† Derived from *catorcista,* which comes from *catorce,* or fourteen, for a member of the 14th of June Movement.

The PRD at the Critical Hour

Trujillo's death did more to heighten than to diminish the fear that pervaded the land. Anti-Trujilloists lived from day to day in dread of a tidal wave of vengeance that would dwarf Trujillo's past crimes. And pro-Trujilloists, both civilian and military, expected that at any minute a popular uprising might sweep over them, wiping out vestiges of the former regime. Those who had neither opposed nor supported Trujillo were just as fearful. No one knew what was going to happen, and everyone expected the worst.

How long the general paralysis produced by this terror would have persisted is impossible to determine, but looking back, it is now fairly obvious that as long as the paralysis lasted, the act of assassinating Trujillo would have remained an isolated occurrence with no effect on the Dominican way of life.

The arrival of the PRD delegation broke the spell of fear that isolated Dominicans from each other and the rest of the world. It gave May 30 a political significance without which it would have been simply an isolated, though heroic, date lost in the memory of a terrible night. Instead, it became the point of departure for a new era of Dominican history. Of the three PRD delegates—Miolán, Castillo, and Silfa—the heaviest political responsibility rested on Miolán. His was a tremendous burden. The fate of an entire population depended on what the party did. And any action it took might easily be misinterpreted by the people or by either of the two distinct forces comprising the government—the civil, headed by Joaquín Balaguer, and the military, headed by Ramfis Trujillo. The PRD delegation did not know to what extent the civilian sector had the upper hand. It was known, however, that the military swarmed with murderers, so any abrupt move by this group would terrify the people. But any indication of satisfaction with that sinister power the PRD delegates might give, could just as easily breed suspicion among the people. The delegates were only too aware that if the people gave Ramfis and his killers an opening, they would take advantage of it to annihilate the three of them.

All of which evokes, certainly not irreverently, the words of Jesus to his disciples: "I send you forth as sheep in the midst of wolves; be ye therefore wise as serpents and harmless as doves." During those first days, it was difficult for the three delegates to assess those who approached, to determine who were Ramfis' thugs or spies and who were the true fighters, who were there to help and who were out to destroy the seed of liberty they were bringing to the country.

The newspapers gave full play to the events of those days, but unprinted were the hushed tensions, the bitter and anxious hours. I had remained outside the country, prepared to mobilize public opinion throughout the continent if anything untoward happened to the delegates. Above all, my task was to raise funds to pay for PRD activities in the Dominican Republic. Thus, I was in a protected position, out of danger, while the three delegates were risking their lives daily. Their heroism deserves their country's gratitude.

With the climate of fear dissipated by the appearance of the PRD, the upper stratum of the Dominican middle class now organized an apolitical patriotic movement called the National Civic Union (Unión Cívica Nacional, or UCN). It was one of those jokes of history, frequent in backward countries like the Dominican Republic, that both the U.S. State Department and the Communist Party supported the formation of the National Civic Union.

The State Department reasoned that as there were no people's political organizations in the Dominican Republic, it was necessary to create one, under the leadership of distinguished and honest men who had demonstrated their loyalty to democratic principles. But the State Department fell into the error of equating opposition to Trujillo with support of democracy, a misconception so widespread throughout the country that even the Communists, well-versed as they were in political and social phenomena, were convinced of it. Of course, the Communists did not share the State Department's aim of buttressing one democratic social sector. Rather, they sought to work inside a democratic organization in order subsequently to capture it from within.

When I, still at my Costa Rica base, learned about the formation of the National Civic Union as an "apolitical patriotic" force, I immediately realized that Communists were involved in it. Although I knew how few Dominican Communists there were, I nevertheless felt that the PRD should act with caution in its dealings with the UCN. On July 15, the PRD held its first rally inside the Dominican Republic. In an address before it, Miolán called for unity among all the people, specifically including the Civic

Union and the 14th of June Movement. This so alarmed me that I telephoned him next day to warn him against making any further bids for unity with the UCN.

Except for the Trujilloists, the only organized political force that had been functioning with any continuity inside the country, at least since 1944, was the clandestine Communist Party. Its propaganda machinery, directed by middle-class youths, was the only one that had been operating regularly. It treated me so mercilessly that I was at a loss to decide who slandered me more thoroughly, Trujillo or the Communists. I was aware that any publicity degrading me, the PRD President, was damaging to the party. If the Communists had infiltrated the National Civic Union—and I was convinced that they had—the UCN would inevitably be hostile to us; moreover, if we joined any alignment including the UCN, the Communists would work against us from within, following the tactic of casting the PRD leaders, including Miolán and myself, in the most unfavorable light before our members.

Thus, we in the PRD had to set about building an invulnerable house with our own hands and our own tools and our own materials. Enough of unity with other parties, enough of confusion. If it was necessary for different political parties to work together on a particular job, we would join in. But unity meant far more than a few leaders cooperating on a specified task. Unity meant supporting a common political line, participating in public gatherings with speakers from different parties who were presenting their views before the same crowds, the establishment of joint committees made up of leaders of the united groups.

Enough of unity—that was our secret slogan. We were a political party, and as such we had initiated our activities in the country. We had clearly stated our purpose. Any shift now would only blur our image as the democratic party of the masses. Our purpose was to organize the great masses of the people and lead them into the political arena, where they could claim and obtain, by democratic procedures, what they had never had—liberty and social justice.

If we joined in a unity movement that included Communists, we would lose our image; furthermore, people would never recognize us as their national leaders.

Nor could we join in an alliance including the upper stratum of the middle class, which rather than a social class, was a caste. Once Trujillo's regime had been liquidated—the process was now under way—our natural adversaries would come from the nucleus of that caste: the first families. They were already active in the National Civic Union, and I knew from the dynamics of Dominican history, that once they had banded together, the next step was inevitable: to convert it into a political party in order to gain the political power that was a prerequisite for acquiring the one thing this group lacked—an economic base. In my opinion, then, the National Civic Union, in spite of the Communists infesting it, was going to end up as a political party.

In July, 1961, in an article published, I believe, the next month, in *Life en Español,* the Latin American edition of *Life* magazine, I wrote: "The dual composition of the National Civic Union is planning in the immediate future to divide the Dominican middle classes into two principal groups, one under the leadership of Dr. [Viriato A.] Fiallo, and the other directed by the engineer [Dr. Manuel] Tavarez [Justo]." I added that "in addition to these two groups, it can quite clearly be predicted that smaller groups among the middle and lower strata of the middle class will be formed in the next few months." Where I used the word "groups," I meant "parties," but I dared not write that lest in Santo Domingo I be condemned for partiality.

In view of the social position occupied by its leaders, any

party formed by the UCN would inevitably become a party of rights, but not necessarily democratic rights. It would probably be rights dedicated to the play for power at all costs. By mid-August, every scrap of news that reached me in Costa Rica indicated that the National Civic Union, though not yet a political party, had begun its drive for power. Three factions were behind this: the first-family caste, the U.S. State Department, and the Communist infiltrators. The only conclusion was that the National Civic Union could take over the government even before becoming a party. And if the UCN did gain control of the government, there would not be substantial departures from the Dominican structure under Trujillo.

The first families had good reason for pressing the UCN to launch its drive for power. They wanted to distribute among themselves the financial legacy left by Trujillo. The State Department wanted the Dominican situation resolved before it degenerated into a total revolution that could follow the course of Cuba's; lifting the sanctions in order to be able to buy Dominican sugar, a matter of great importance to the U.S. Government and to businessmen and financiers involved in the sugar market, was only part of the story. For the Communists entrenched within it, a UCN seizure of power, although it would represent only partial power for them, would guarantee that the Communist movement would not be disbanded and persecuted.

The presence of Communists at the core of the National Civic Union was a secret, even to U.S. representatives in the Dominican Republic. But an experienced politician knows that whenever an "apolitical patriotic" movement is organized, there are Communists in it. All peoples respond to the appeal for apolitical patriotism; there is no better formula for rallying and organizing the masses.

It would have been difficult for the PRD to block a

power play by a movement that would ultimately show its right-wing leanings. According to our conclusions, even the Communists, with all their cleverness in manipulating organizations, would be unable to deflect the UCN's radicalization to the right, because the Communists lacked the support of the masses.

After various consultations, Miolán and I decided that the only course of action open to the PRD was to make the revolution from a position of power, or at least to start the revolution from above. This could be accomplished only if we surrounded President Balaguer with a Cabinet drawn from the UCN, the 14th of June Movement, and the PRD. With such a Cabinet, it was conceivable that we could accomplish in three months what the revolutionary Cuban Government of Ramón Grau San Martín had achieved in 1933. This was the only solution in sight. In historical terms, our country stood more or less at the level of Cuba in 1933.

Balaguer had made favorable statements about a similar plan. And so in September I went to Miami for an interview with Emilio Rodríguez Demorizi, Balaguer's representative. From Miami I went to Washington for discussions with a few State Department officials and a number of UCN representatives. This was the Dominican Revolutionary Party's first contact with the U.S. State Department. Nevertheless, at a party rally on June 14, 1962, Dr. Manuel Tavarez Justo was to charge that the PRD had been sent to the Dominican Republic as an agent of the U.S. State Department. This was not only unjust to us, but a flat contradiction of the historical truth. Actually, the Civic Union was the State Department's favored organization. The UCN had permanent agents assigned to Washington, and frequently sent representatives to Washington.

When I arrived in Washington, the UCN had just published a manifesto that set forth its program of action—a collegiate government empowered to contract international obligations and, of course, the dissolution of the Balaguer government; in short, a Council of State. My impression was that the State Department had collaborated in formulating this, and consequently that it supported the UCN. Thus, there could be no support in Washington for a national coalition government that could bring about the revolution quickly from the top. It only remained, then, for me to return at long last to the Dominican Republic and work there for a solution.

The idea of a revolution from the top was feasible in spite of the presence of Ramfis Trujillo, with his court of murderers, in the Armed Forces' headquarters. Ramfis was the son of Rafael Leonidas, but he was not and could never be Rafael Leonidas. A Cabinet that would carry out revolutionary measures would strengthen civil power and would gain popular support for that civil power. If, in addition, that Cabinet had foreign backing—a political factor so important that neither the United States nor Russia, despite their being the world's most powerful nations, can afford to dispense with it—such a Cabinet could oust Ramfis from his post as Commander in Chief of the Armed Forces.

But this plan for a Cabinet that could execute a revolution from the top collapsed when viewed from inside the country. Between August and September, the Civic Union strengthened its hold on the middle class, which took the lead in the political battle being waged on the streets. Thereby, the popular aims of the battle (or what should have been its popular aims)—a revolution to transform the country's economic, social, and political structures and put them at the service of the people—were astutely converted into purely personal anti-Trujilloist terms. Its goals were scaled down to merely a change in the cast. Trujillo had been removed from the scene, and after him, the Trujilloists had disappeared, since they could not survive without the human factor of Trujillo's leadership. But the Trujilloist structures and systems remained. *They* were what needed to be changed.

Immediately after my arrival in the country on October 20—for the first time in twenty-four years—I held discussions with leaders of the 14th of June Movement, among them Dr. Manuel Tavarez Justo, and of the Civic Union, headed by Dr. Viriato A. Fiallo. Point by point, I outlined for them the PRD proposal to form a government of national unity that could in the least possible time effect a revolution from the top. Neither the Catorcitas nor the UCN was receptive to the plan, and since the PRD could not undertake it alone, we had to abandon it.

We turned now to a long-range effort to develop a political consciousness in the people so that they themselves could launch their peaceful democratic revolution. But educating the people would take many months, perhaps years. In adopting this approach, we were admitting that the opportunity to quickly execute a revolution from the top would probably never come again.

The key word was "quickly." What a revolutionary government, with every instrument of power in its hands, can accomplish in three months is beyond the scope of a normal government, with all the instruments of power, public and private, reserved to their respective spheres.

The Dominican Republic's opportunity for a bloodless revolution existed only in the final months of 1961. The critical year that had begun on May 30 with Trujillo's death was uncertain enough already, but no one had any notion of what might take place in the country thereafter.

It was now the last week of October, and I had arrived in the country on the twentieth. The Dominican Revolutionary Party was spreading, to the east and to the south, but it was obvious that the National Civic Union dominated articulate public opinion. The masses still had no voice in forming public opinion. The common people—the great rural masses and the urban slum dwellers—were at the edge of the battlefield, on which National Civic Union forces were opposing Balaguer's government. The people distrusted and feared the UCN.

In those days, articulate public opinion was made up of the middle class, particularly the upper and middle strata. One can say, without exaggeration, that by the end of October, 1961, there were fewer than a dozen PRD members in the middle class, and not one of these in its upper stratum.

Despite hard work by Miolán and others in the first Provisional Executive Committee of the Party, the people from the cities and villages had responded to the UCN slogan of the "anti-Trujilloist struggle" rather than to the PRD's struggle for social justice, individual liberty, and well-being for the masses. Moreover, Ramfis Trujillo had loosed a campaign of terror against our party, destroying homes and breaking bones. On the very night before my arrival in the country, a group of his henchmen had attacked my sister's home, which was to be my official residence. That same day, some thugs had invaded the home of Francisco Gómez Estrella, Secretary of Rural Affairs for the party's Executive Committee, and systematically reduced it to rubble. Not a stick of furniture, not a lamp, not a door or a window was intact, and Gómez Estrella and his son were brutally beaten; a year later, the father was still under a doctor's care.

iii

Misguided Youth

The 14th of June Movement had been formed secretly around the end of 1959, with a mystique of heroism and sacrifice that was responsible for many martyrs, much torture in Trujillo's prisons, and many missing persons whose graves have never been found.

In its first year and a half, a 14th of June cell sprang up in almost every Dominican village. The chiefs and members of these secret cells were young students and professionals of the upper and middle strata of the middle class, along with a few, but very few, from its lower stratum.

These young people were fired by patriotic fervor, they were honest, and they were good fighters. But they had not had time to study the people and thus were not familiar with the country's social make-up. They did not know the difference in attitude toward life between a farmer and a rich man's son from the capital, between a sugar worker and a lawyer, between an unemployed man from Gualey and an Embassy Secretary. Under Trujillo's dictatorship, the Republic had lived isolated from the rest of the world.

Anti-Trujilloist fighters in the interior did not know the thinking of those who had managed to leap over the wall and get out to other worlds, where they had been able to study more calmly and with relative objectivity the Dominican historical process, the national psychology, the play of internal and external forces that had formed—or deformed —the Dominican people over the centuries.

The Dominican Republic was outside the mainstream of the rest of the Americas. Historically, it had fallen out of step with them. The Americas, as a whole, had one rhythm, and the Dominican Republic had another. Among the many resulting disadvantages to our country was an information gap in a wide range of subjects. We Dominicans had not made studies—or even observations—of our own social make-up, our national psychology, and the characteristics of our social groups. And it had never occurred to us to use modern methods of historical analysis in interpreting national events.

The Catorcitas, organized and operating inside the country, were working in the dark. They had appeared on the Dominican scene amid secrecy and political prisons. They failed to realize that no human being escapes his environment and did not understand that they had not remained free of the influence of the Dominican scene.

The Dominican Communist Party, called the Popular Socialist Party (Partido Socialista Popular, or PSP), had functioned legally in Santo Domingo until 1945. Trujillo had permitted this in order to demonstrate that there were Communists in the country and that he, and only he, could exterminate them. This was so that he could declare himself the leading anti-Communist of the Americas, a title quite necessary if he was to assure himself Washington's backing. The remaining members of the Popular Socialist Party had secretly continued operating after the dispersal of its leaders in 1945, and had sought to infiltrate the young

Catorcitas. The Communists became so audacious that they got not only their propaganda but their propagandists as well into La Victoria Prison, which held most of the Catorcitas who had fallen into the hands of the Trujilloist political police. In this manner the Communists managed to infiltrate among some of the Catorcitas.

The flank of the 14th of June Movement most vulnerable to Communist penetration was the nationalism of the Catorcitas. Nationalism had disappeared in the rest of Dominicans. Nowhere else in the world had there ever been a population more apathetic than the Dominicans since 1930. The upper stratum of the middle class, particularly, spent the years under Trujillo waiting for U.S. Marines to solve the national problem by landing one day and heaving him out of power. Trujillo, well aware of this attitude, set out to demonstrate to his country that he had the all-out backing of the United States. He went so far as to christen one avenue "George Washington," another "Cordell Hull," and another "U.S. Marine Corps." But when it came to his personal interests, he held the United States at a safe distance.

The nationalism of the Catorcitas was a consequence of their anti-Trujilloism, and manifested itself as anti-Americanism. If Trujillo and the United States were allied, the young Catorcitas reasoned, then it was proper to be anti-American.

In Santo Domingo there existed a phenomenon of social psychology that in any other country would have been virtually incomprehensible. An entire generation had been born and had grown up under Trujilloism, never knowing any other political system. For any Dominican under thirty, this thing called democracy had to be the same in every other country as it was in his own. If in the Dominican Republic nothing happened—as, surely, nothing *could* happen—without an order from its dictator, then the same situation must exist in the United States. Thus, when an American newspaper or Congressman or Ambassador lauded Trujillo, it was thought, logically enough, that the spokesman represented the feeling of the United States Government. Of course, Trujillo had such rigid control of the press, radio, and television that no other sort of statement by anyone from the United States would have been circulated anyway. Headlines trumpeted any favorable U.S. comment on the regime, even if it came from a simple tourist without the vaguest notion of what he represented in the eyes of the Dominican people.

It was easy enough, then, for agents of the Popular Socialist Party to channel the nationalism of young Catorcitas into hostility toward the United States. And the natural enemies of the 14th of June later made use of this attitude to present them as dangerous Communists to priests, the military, businessmen, and other upper-middle class groups. But before reaching this point, the 14th of June Movement was simply used by the PSP, like a new suit by a man trying to make a good impression and obtain the job he seeks.

The first families in the Dominican Republic were not a class but a caste. In the last days of Trujillo's regime, even before the dictator was shot to death, that caste aspired to become a class. To achieve this, it had to acquire the economic base it had always lacked. The first families had learned a lesson from Trujillo: Once in power, it is easy enough to become as rich as the country's industry and finance allow. This concept is quite different from the old-fashioned values of another time in history, when wealth was measured in lands or cattle.

The first-family caste had been traditionally an arrogant social group because its members gained entree by birth, not by economic or political power. But in the economic and political areas, they were dependent and therefore weak, which explains why they submitted to Trujillo, who did not come from that caste.

During Trujillo's last years, a few first families had given up their political activities—which they had become involved in through Trujillo—and with the dictator's support, had applied themselves to industry or enriched themselves by collecting commissions from those who did business with the government. The moment had now come for the caste to achieve class status, and they instinctively recognized it. From that time until Trujillo's death, they worked to organize a political group with which to launch their drive for power, since power was indispensable to a rapid leap into the class category. That group was the National Civic Union.

Once organized, the National Civic Union found there was no sector of the population toward which it could direct itself except the youth from basically the same social circle, and that youth comprised the Catorcita. The historic moment came at a really critical point when parents had to identify themselves as reactionaries and their children as revolutionaries. By this time, the PRD movement was under way, addressing the masses with a message of social and economic transformation, which was to lay the groundwork for a future revolution. The nascent forces of reaction spoke a merely political language, the language of appearances, but the Catorcita youth, which should have been wholly revolutionary, allowed itself to be mesmerized by that language.

The UCN employed two arguments in order to win over the Catorcitas—that the UCN was an apolitical, patriotic body of national unity that would be dissolved the moment the Trujillo family's power was destroyed, and that it would be headed by a man of stature, a man who had never joined Trujillo's party, Dr. Viriato A. Fiallo.

When the hour came to make their political decision,

these young people reacted not as revolutionaries, but as sons of first families; they were true to the caste in which they had been born and reared. Additional factors influenced them: the activities of the Communist Popular Socialist Party, its anti-American propaganda and its campaign to discredit the PRD leaders by making them appear to be American agents of long standing, as well as the lowest of political adventurers.

In the eyes of the Catorcita nucleus, we in the PRD were a species of moral leper. On the other hand, the Civic Union appeared to be the ultimate in patriotic, anti-Trujilloist integrity. If Dr. Fiallo became head of the UCN, the Catorcita leaders could not doubt that the UCN would be an impeccable, honorable organization. And if Dr. Fiallo said that the UCN would be patriotic and apolitical, that it would be dissolved once the fight against the Trujillo family was won, so it would be. In October of 1959, in the Introduction to *Trujillo: Reasons for an Unparalleled Tyranny,* I had observed: "When acting in a political capacity, men are neither good nor evil; they are the product of the forces that made them and that sustain them, and with certain frequency are either playthings of those forces or are their beneficiaries." But this simple notion, long familiar in the political world, was something Dominicans did not know. The Catorcitas—and the Communists who had infiltrated the UCN—believed in Dr. Fiallo because he was one of their own social group. None realized that Dr. Fiallo would have to go along with his caste, whether or not he wanted to, and that it planned to use the National Civic Union as a political instrument with which to seize power.

The leaders of the 14th of June, some issuing directives from their jail cells, gave orders for all members to join the Civic Union. And so the UCN was born against the clandestine backdrop of the 14th of June. A few months later, when the UCN decided to declare itself a political party and no longer simply a patriotic organization, many Catorcita leaders who now figured in the UCN command renounced the 14th of June and remained in the Civic Union.

With the push given by Catorcita youth, the prestige of Dr. Fiallo, and the anti-Trujilloist campaign—which amounted to accusing anyone in opposition of Trujilloist affiliations—the National Civic Union in a short time forged ahead. I watched this gigantic national fraud, and I was alarmed. But it was impossible to open the eyes of those middle-class young people, whose ranks now were rapidly being swelled by new members from the lower stratum of the middle class, even a few from the working class. They were spurred by their resentments, their bitter memories of tortures and humiliations suffered under Trujilloism. The only thing we could do was to work to keep the great poor masses from also falling into the trap, by continuing our campaign to form a national revolutionary consciousness.

By August, the Civic Union had conceived a plan to gain power by the creation of a Council of State made up of its own men. The UCN understood that once on the battlefield, the PRD could be a powerful enemy, but now it considered the PRD unimportant.

Combating the PRD was a relatively simple matter. In the Dominican Republic, anyone who did not belong to the first families did not have prestige, and we, the PRD leaders, were not from the first families. In Santo Domingo, a man could possess integrity, but if he did not belong to the caste, his virtue would be unknown and thus it could easily be denied and destroyed in the public's eyes by slander manufactured in the circle of the first families. He could be intelligent, but the public could be persuaded that intelligence was dangerous because he was a rogue or had the qualities of a rogue. Public opinion was formed by gossip, rumors, slander, *double-entendres,* and even mocking nicknames. It had always been this way in the Dominican Republic, and so it was still, toward the end of 1961.

Those who read the UCN and 14th of June newspapers published between August, 1961, and August, 1962—especially those published between November, 1961, and July, 1962—will find proof of what I say. In the Catorcita weekly, *Claridad,* and in the Civic Union paper, no insult was spared me, Miolán, or the PRD. We were the worst, lowest, and cheapest crooked politicians in the Caribbean, worse even than Trujilloists and the bums who had sold out to Washington.

The Dominican Revolutionary Party won the 1962 elections by a rousing majority of roughly two to one over the UCN. Despite this, we had taken power without even managing to acquire that indescribable but potent aura called prestige. During the days of our government, and for many months after the coup that threw us out of power, the most frequent accusation against us was that we had surrounded ourselves with "garbage," that our Cabinet lacked "high-class" men. All of this merely meant that our Cabinet included none of the elite, that our high officials were not from the first families. I was so conscious of this caste hatred for people outside it that between October, 1961, when I returned to the Dominican Republic, and September 25, 1963, when I was taken prisoner in the National Palace by perpetrators of the coup, I did not visit the National University a single time; I knew that its student body was under the influence of the first families. This elite tried to deny me even my nationality. For it, I was not even a Dominican.

Nevertheless, within three or four months at the most, the situation began to change. After Trujillo's death, the people were ready, finally, to stop being spectators at their own drama and mount the stage as actors, and that is what the PRD did. It made the people actors in the national drama. From the beginning, the PRD put the problem facing the people into social and economic terms, and the masses recognized the PRD as their natural spokesman in the area of politics. Thus, while we were being discredited among the elite, the masses were swelling our membership.

Even six months after the elections—when the PRD had been functioning in the country for almost a year, and I was speaking daily on the radio, and our political conduct, free from subterfuge of any kind, spoke for itself—the Catorcitas still pursued the course laid out by the UCN. The saddest part of the matter was that they were acting in all honesty, in the best of faith, convinced that they were serving the Dominican revolution, that they were working to rid the nation of unprincipled politicians of the worst sort.

Of course, given the social and political backwardness of the country, it was very foolish to expect the middle-class youth to join us in our campaign to enroll the masses in the cause of a democratic revolution. We had to continue plowing without the oxen the historical moment demanded. The Dominican democratic revolution could not be achieved during the one juncture when it was possible— that is, at the end of the dramatic year of 1961.

There was a final chance, at the moment the Trujillos fled the country. But by then the deflection accomplished by the Civic Union's clever campaign was so evident that only madmen would have attempted to seize that opportunity.

As for the Communist groups, by the end of 1961 they were small, had little influence, and docilely accepted the slogans of the UCN. Key leaders of the outlawed Popular Socialist Party were in exile, and the smaller Communist group, the Popular Dominican Movement (Movimiento

Popular Dominicano, or MPD), which had been operating in the country since its legalization by Trujillo around 1960, had neither a definite political line nor sufficient members. By its own definition, it was Marxist-Leninist-Fidelist, but in reality it smacked more of anarchism than anything else. From the outset, it had been locked in a fight to the death with the PSP, because of personal feuds between leaders of the two parties.

The "Patriots" and Their Plans

On the day of my arrival in Santo Domingo, the young people from the Ciudad Nueva (New City) neighborhood had a scuffle with the police. These youths—Catorcitas, Communists, members of the MPD, or belonging to no group—made up the Civic Union's direct action vanguard. They fought against the police because they thought the national struggle ought to take place in the political area. None of them believed that solutions ought to be sought in the economic and social fields. On the other hand, young people from the highland districts of Gualey and Guachupita, sons of laborers and the unemployed, ran to surround my car—and to push it when the motor gave out near the Duarte Bridge—meanwhile chanting rhythmically: "Juan Bo has come! Now it will be done!"

What did they want done?

They wanted to be lifted out of the misery and the hopelessness into which the Trujillo family had plunged them. At that moment, the Trujillos held all the military power, which rested in the hands of the ex-dictator's first-born son, the young Ramfis. A casual observer might think that they also held all the political power, officially in the hands of Joaquín Balaguer. In the eyes of those who could not see past events to the forces that controlled them, Trujilloism seemed intact. But such was not the case, because Trujilloism could not exist without Trujillo. His regime was dead. What Dominicans were witnessing was its burial. Nevertheless, Dominican politicians were so blind to the facts that when I stated, on the afternoon of my arrival and again during the days that followed, that the Trujillos would remain in power only six weeks more—"between three and six weeks" were my exact words—even my colleagues among the PRD leaders thought I had lost my mind. Ramfis left the country on November 18, and on the nineteenth, a month after my arrival in the Dominican Republic, the parade into exile of his uncles and the rest of his relatives began. I had not lost my mind.

In the four weeks between my arrival in the country and the Trujillos' exit, the Dominican middle class lived in a state of constant agitation. But the masses, especially in the urban slum areas, were not affected by it. The object of the agitation was not Ramfis Trujillo, at least it did not appear to be; the object was President Balaguer. Little was said of Ramfis and his entourage of killers. But there was endless talk about Balaguer, who was being asked to relinquish power.

In a matter of days, one could feel the pressure build. Youths from the UCN took matters into their hands. They destroyed every street lamp in sight, using children's slingshots with incredible accuracy. They broke store windows and provoked riots. During the night, the lower- and lower-middle-class neighborhoods resounded with an urgent beating on cans calculated to communicate the agitation through reflex actions. Telephone wires hummed endlessly, transmitting rumors, watchwords, and gossip. Radio stations constantly incited the people to violence. A holy war against Balaguer was preached at rallies and in the newspapers published by the UCN and the 14th of June. But nothing was said about reform, and that was all the masses cared about. Only the PRD held fast to its reform goals, and only the PRD did not preach hatred. The PRD was interested in social and economic reform, even if it was Balaguer who put it into effect—and if possible, it would be Balaguer, since, in our opinion, the people could not wait—because the PRD was out not for power but rather for changes that would benefit the great masses.

The National Civic Union acted in such a way, and with such persistence and shrewdness, that when the Trujillo family was finally ousted, hatred against Balaguer had been injected into the upper and middle strata of the middle class and into a large part of its lower stratum. The result was that these social groups demanded an immediate change—but merely a change of men, a superficial change. In a few brief months, Trujilloism had been replaced with Fialloism, and we had only gone from one kind of bossism to another. The middle class felt that the evils of the government originated not in the system but in the man, and it had the idea that exchanging Balaguer for another man —as long as he was a private citizen—would improve matters.

At the beginning of November, Dr. Luis Manuel Baquero, Secretary General of the UCN, appeared at my house with the news that it had been arranged for the presidents and secretaries general of the UCN, 14th of June, and PRD parties to make a trip to Washington for the ostensible purpose of appealing to the OAS not to lift the sanctions imposed against the Dominican Republic in August, 1960. Baquero explained that the real reason would be to reach an agreement with the State Department on how to bring an end to the Balaguer-Ramfis regime—

but that this information would be kept from the 14th of June. I told Baquero that although I would discuss the matter with my colleagues, I was not in favor of going to Washington or any place else. I explained that with the situation inside the country, compounded by the international pressure, I expected that the powder keg might go off any day. And when it did, the national leaders must be inside, not outside, the country, because one could predict where events would lead. When Baquero left, I asked Miolán to come to my home and discuss the situation with me. He was still there when Fiallo's eldest son appeared to repeat the invitation. We told him No, and we were right. The following day, the UCN's Fiallo and Baquero, and Guzmán and Tavarez Justo of the 14th of June left for the United States, and so the flight of the Trujillo family caught them outside the country.

Balaguer had arranged for Ramfis Trujillo to get his uncles Negro and Petán out of the country. However, Washington made it clear that the sanctions would not be lifted until Ramfis himself left the country, whereupon the dictator's son called back his uncles and all three went into hiding on a Dominican warship. On learning of this surreptitious return, the PRD Executive Committee held an urgent meeting. We came to the conclusion that the reappearance of his uncles would precipitate Ramfis' departure as Armed Forces leader, and that this in turn would create a vacuum in the military command. Who would fill this vacuum, and how? That was a difficult question for even the wisest oracle. That night, on the quarter-hour radio program that I conducted as spokesman of the PRD, I made a statement that won instant popularity: "We have stumbled, but he who stumbles and does not fall makes progress."

The first thing next morning, a PRD delegation went to talk with Balaguer. I do not recall how many of us were in that delegation, but I am certain that Angel Miolán and Humbertilio Valdez Sánchez, another Executive Committee member, accompanied me. We told Balaguer that we believed the return of the Trujillo uncles would pull down their nephew Ramfis with them.

"It has already happened," Balaguer said. "He sent me his resignation this morning."

I asked Balaguer if he could depend on any officers of the Armed Forces or of the police to give him support in the event of a military uprising.

"Not one," he said. "I do not even know the officers they send here to the Palace to guard me."

His situation was indeed difficult. The vacuum left by Ramfis would inevitably stir up the barracks, and no one— not even Balaguer, the President of the Republic—knew who would emerge from the commotion as the new military leader. No one knew if this man would destroy civil power, deliver it into the UCN's hands, or retain it himself. Anything was possible, and we found ourselves practically without means to meet whatever might present itself. Perhaps we were faced with the last chance for a revolution. But the masses do not organize, direct, or launch revolutions. This is done by a minority, and in Latin America today, that minority is the youth of the middle class. The Dominican Revolutionary Party had the masses, though not as many as it was to have a year later. However, it did not have the middle class, and more particularly, it did not have the youth of the middle class. And at this point, in November, 1961, the masses in the PRD were incapable of revolutionary action.

Out of this confusion, General Pedro Rafael Rodríguez Echavarría, head of the Santiago Air Base, emerged suddenly as the military leader. Rodríguez Echavarría though unpolished and hot-tempered, frankly desired social justice. He had no idea how to achieve it, but he felt it was necessary. Of course, he was a typical soldier, with all the vices of his calling, and had begun his career as a common soldier. By virtue of his simple background, he was anti-UCN. Like the masses he came from, he instinctively repudiated the upper caste that had crawled out of the Trujilloist ruins and now wanted to wrest control of the country.

On the afternoon of November 18, when Rodríguez Echavarría's uprising in Santiago was believed to be imminent, Miolán, Valdez Sánchez, and I were in the Hotel Embajador, in Santo Domingo, for a conference. Someone said that Rodríguez Echavarría considered the PRD an enemy, that he had ordered an assault made on PRD headquarters in Santiago a few days before—in which local PRD leaders had been treated brutally—and that he had said that if he got hold of me he would yank my head off because he thought I was a Communist. I knew this was typical Dominican gossip. At the Embajador, I soon began getting telephone calls, and from the way the callers spoke, I gathered that they were soldiers. Each delivered almost the identical message: "Don Juan, get out of town. They are planning to kill you."

But these calls could not be connected with Rodríguez Echavarría, because they originated in the capital, not Santiago. Ramfis Trujillo, his uncles, and his retinue of killers were still in the capital, but Rodríguez Echavarría was in Santiago. Friends, among them a U.S. official, repeatedly urged Miolán and me to go home and get ready to flee the country again if it seemed advisable. But we refused. We were the only political leaders left in the country, and we could not abandon the people amid such confusion, which could turn into tragedy at any moment.

Rodríguez Echavarría supported Balaguer as President of the Republic. Now freed from the Trujillos, Balaguer acted, though timidly, to reduce the economic and social oppression of the masses. The Dominican countryside was a study in misery. Nowhere else in the Americas, with the exception of Haiti, was there so much hunger, so many rags hanging on so many undernourished bodies, so many wretched farms.

Perhaps those who had spent all their lives in the Dominican Republic were blind to such misery, but we who had returned from exile in Venezuela, Mexico, Costa Rica—in fact, any place else in Latin America—were horrified. Before my return, Miolán had warned me that I must expect the worst, that only by the furthest stretch of the imagination could I conceive of the hunger rampant in our land. He had been right. The Republic had lost far more than the thirty-one years spanned by the dictatorship. In many respects, it was living in the mid-nineteenth century, but with the added problems of the twentieth century. In fact, as I was able to observe for myself later, many Dominicans still lived in the eighteenth century.

The country needed a revolution to bring it up to at least the twentieth century. Not a revolution Cuban style à la Fidel Castro, but a revolution Cuban style à la Grau San Martín; a revolution that would permit us to advance in a few months to at least the point Venezuela reached in 1945, when Betancourt first came to power. This would be almost a dream come true.

Rodríguez Echavarría supported Balaguer as President of the Republic, and that determined the position of the Civic Union toward the General. Despite his nationalist feelings, which were as strong as his instinct for social justice, the Catorcita youth opposed Rodríguez Echavarría, since they followed the UCN political line. Rodríguez Echavarría himself was inclined toward the 14th of June policies.

Beginning on November 19, 1961, the UCN was to dedicate all its strength to overthrowing both Balaguer and

Rodríguez Echavarría. U.S. representatives were working openly toward that end. Arturo Morales Carrión, Under Secretary of State for Latin America, flew in from Washington and moved into the U.S. Embassy. Jordi Brossa, J. Donald Reid Cabral, Luis Manuel Baquero, and practically every other key man in the Civic Union visited the Embassy so often that it appeared that they, too, had set up residence there. During the three or four times I was a dinner guest there, on the invitation of Morales Carrión, or the Consul General, John Calvin Hill, Jr., I saw UCN leaders trot in and out, unannounced, and make small talk as if in their own homes.

I then understood that the State Department required events in the Dominican Republic to be under control. In the unstable situation following the liquidation of the most ruthless dictatorship on record in the Americas, and with the Cuban example on one side, Washington suddenly did not want to be faced with an unchecked revolutionary flood. If the dominant force in the country was the Civic Union, it was logical for the State Department to feel that by controlling the Civic Union, it could more or less relax. But I could not understand how a Dominican group could bind itself to be faithful to a policy dictated by a power that of necessity had its own objectives independent of those that Dominicans ought to seek.

U.S. intentions could very well be legitimate in terms of U.S. interests. The United States is a great nation, with worldwide influence and worldwide obligations, and in 1961 it was experiencing the unhappy reality of being the loser of a great political and diplomatic battle to a tiny Antilles island-nation called Cuba. It was certainly not about to lose another battle in the Dominican Republic. But the interests of the Dominican people were not those of the United States, any more than they were those of Russia or Cuba or any other country. The Dominican people needed to find for themselves the solutions for their own anguish, the road that would lead them to dignity, liberty, and well-being. And that road would not be pointed out by the United States or anyone else who wanted to impose a formula that did not emerge from the hearts of our own people and our own history. We of the PRD, as I said one night to Morales Carrión, were not going to conspire to overthrow Balaguer. We believed in the people, and the people, the mass, had no stake in these maneuvers.

In November, 1961, and even in December, and January, 1962, the Dominican Republic was the scene of one of the world's most flagrant political ironies: The National Civic Union had the full backing of the U.S. Embassy—but its action groups were Communists from the PSP and young nationalists from the 14th of June. Without knowing it, the nationalists and the Communists were acting in concert with the United States. As was to be seen later, almost the entire District Committee of the UCN was controlled by PSP members; the labor movement organized by the UCN was in the same straits.

The Communists, the MPD, and the 14th of June instigated the general strike called in December with the aim of toppling Balaguer and Rodríguez Echavarría. The people, the great masses, took no part in the strike. In fact, they turned against it. The strike had been decided on at a meeting that Miolán and I attended as representatives of the PRD. A gentleman with the mentality of a mid-eighteenth-century Spanish colonial official stated that the UCN had to make Balaguer feel its strength. "That means a general strike," I whispered to Miolán. And so it did. That night the strike was resolved upon.

The PRD, over my radio program, announced that it was not backing the strike. By taking this position, the PRD at one stroke earned the sympathy of the great masses from the slums and farms, and the mortal hatred of the

UCN. That strike marked a crucial moment in the existence of the PRD. If we had not faithfully hewed to our line, the PRD would have been weakened, perhaps fatally. But we understod the people, and they us; we spoke the same language. We listened to their heart; we understood its desires and its anguishes. From that December strike, the party emerged strengthened. By the end of the month, our membership passed 120,000. Moreover, the strike marked a turning point in the attitude of the masses toward the Civic Union: Until then they had shown indifference to Civic Union propaganda; now they became frankly hostile to it.

This was the first harvest of the seeds sown by the PRD. In that month, the masses began to straighten backs that had been bent double throughout Dominican history. If their mood continued, the day would come when the people would rise to their full height, and begin shaping their nation's history. When would that day come? We had no way of knowing, but we were sure that it would come.

On December 13 and 14, the UCN leaders held a meeting during which they decided to convert their organization into a political party. The immediate consequence of that was a campaign to discredit the PRD and its leaders. It was clear that as a political party, the UCN would have to combat the PRD, which from its inception had presented itself to the people as a political party.

When written proof of the agreement to convert the UCN to a political party came into my hands, my associates on the Executive Committee asserted that it would be proper for me, as party spokesman, to denounce the move publicly. But I replied that the middle class had such faith in Fiallo that if I said that he had agreed to converting the UCN into a party, with himself as its leader, I would be branded a slanderer and we would lose prestige. This view prevailed and events proved its wisdom. I reasoned that it would be better for the people suddenly to learn that the UCN had become a party, with Fiallo as its leader, and that the announcement should come from Fiallo himself. "He will be stripped naked before the public," I said, and explained that Dominican middle-class psychology being what it is, the UCN's deception in heretofore portraying itself as apolitical would be fatal. I felt that the UCN, which was already beginning to lose some of its following, would rapidly decline until it would no longer be the country's principal political organization.

And so it happened. In the seven months between Trujillo's death and December 31, 1961, Dominican history hurtled forward, devouring, creating, destroying, and rebuilding. Not in vain are the power to create and the power to destroy conjoined in the human species.

The "Patriots" Come to Power

After the Trujillos had fled, the country entered a period that was openly revolutionary in feeling, though not in action. Soldiers sent to protect the property of the vanished Trujillos and pro-Trujilloists took what they wanted and called in the mob to pick over the leavings. The notion of authority had been replaced by that of popular vengeance, which at first was appeased by plundering the property of those who had fled. Everywhere—in the large cities, especially the capital, and throughout the countryside—gangs ran wild sacking property, burning houses, knocking down fences, and carrying off furniture, cattle, horses, doors, windows. Soldiers and police joined in with the people and grabbed their share of the booty.

This was the primitive reaction of some of the masses, who wanted to get what they could out of the fall of the Trujillo regime. They should have been able to find their rewards through a democratic revolution that would have reshaped the social structure so as to benefit everybody.

The masses were looking for bonuses and took them in furniture and dishes.

In a way, they were right. A quick revolution was impossible. The Civic Union had channeled all the national sentiment for a revolution into simple anti-Trujilloism, a battle against what had been, not against what still was. And Trujilloism was not what had to be fought now. Trujilloism had been something evil that belonged to the past. What had to be fought was in the present: the nation's social and economic structure, more backward than that in any other Latin American country, and the harsh inequalities of all kinds. The UCN had acted like the bullfighter, working the bull with arrogant skill, guiding it behind the *muleta* to save himself from a fatal goring.

Won over by the UCN's preaching, the middle-class youth—the Catorcitas and even the Communists, the MPD's and even the handful of Social Christians there were in those days—shouted demands that Balaguer and Rodríguez Echavarría resign. But none of these youths offered the people any kind of program, any list of steps to be taken by the government that replaced Balaguer's. The spectacle was sad to behold for those of us who realized that this was the last opportunity for a Dominican revolution. It was even sadder because there was no way now to put these maliciously misdirected people back on course. Those youths, believing in good faith that what they were working for in their forthright manner constituted a revolution, were wholeheartedly serving the enemies of the revolution.

The pressure on Balaguer was building up. One day at the end of December, he let me know that he was buckling under it, that he would have to give up the presidency. Between the Civic Union and the PRD, he preferred to turn over his power to the latter, he said. Shortly afterward, on a Sunday morning, General Rodríguez Echavarría called me and invited me to talk with him at the Military

Club. There he told me that President Balaguer wanted to name me Minister of the Armed Forces, whereupon he would immediately resign the presidency, and I, as Minister of the Armed Forces, would automatically become President under the Constitution. "If you accept, I shall resign my post, and if you choose to name me Minister of the Armed Forces once you are in office, well and good," the General said. "But if you prefer someone else, that is entirely up to you. In any case, I assure you of the loyalty of the Armed Forces."

I had not yet given him my answer when an aide arrived to inform him that Balaguer wanted him on the telephone. The General left, and returned a few moments later to tell me that a meeting had been held in the Palace, and that Morales Carrión was asking Balaguer for an immediate resolution of the political crisis. The General left for the Palace before I could explain my reaction to his request.

Things were coming to a head. If I accepted the presidency from Balaguer, middle-class youth would react violently. They felt that the UCN must come to power. The choice, as they saw it, was not between revolution and no revolution, but between Trujilloism and anti-Trujilloism. They did not realize that at the root of their feeling was the desire to avenge themselves for their humiliations, tortures, and sufferings under Trujillo, and that because of this feeling they had been cleverly diverted from the revolution.

Furthermore, the PRD did not have sufficient strength to maintain itself in power, and the Armed Forces were not bound to the PRD as they had been to Balaguer. Politically, Balaguer had been born and reared in Trujillo's shadow, and the military leaders respected him as Trujillo's political heir. Congress, also Trujillo's creation, would not be as responsive to the PRD as it had been to Balaguer. Although Balaguer had the best intentions, he did not realize that a government would be the prisoner of Trujillo's political machinery, which remained intact, and that at the same time it would feel the full weight of the opposition of the middle class that Balaguer had also felt, but a hundred times stronger because of the UCN middle class's wrath at what they would consider a mockery and a deception directed against them.

The following day General Rodríguez Echavarría telephoned me several times without reaching me. He was after a quick decision. When he finally got me, it was late afternoon. I told him that there was no point in either my, his, or Balaguer's pursuing the matter. That night, on the quarter-hour PRD radio program, I used for the first time a phrase that I was to repeat frequently: "The PRD will accept power only from the hands of the people." I am sure that few listeners understood what was behind those words.

By this time, UCN and 14th of June propaganda was rampant, depicting the PRD as a Trujilloist party tied to Balaguer. From one end of the country to the other, UCN youth action groups painted a little palm—the symbol of Trujillo's party—over the "R" in our party initials on every PRD poster they could find. Thus it appeared: "P-palm-D," suggesting Partido Dominicano (or Dominican Party), the name of the party that Trujillo had established and maintained as the only party throughout his rule. Out of the UCN offices daily poured dozens of slogans, which the young party members repeated wherever they went; all were slanderous and designed to picture PRD leaders as agents of Ramfis and his uncle Petán, recipients of funds from Balaguer and the ousted Trujilloists.

Alarmed by these attacks, my fellow members of the PRD Executive Committee begged me to answer them with a broadcast statement. I took a different position. I was convinced that the Dominican middle class was not reaching the masses, had no knowledge of their psychology, and had no notion of their objectives. What was worse, the middle class did not understand the language of the masses, nor did the masses understand the language of the middle class. The middle class, owing to its peculiar psychological nature, cannot exist without its daily ration of gossip. It is a constant font of gossip. It creates and consumes gossip. (When I was President, I once said that the major national industry was gossip.) But the masses—the unemployed, the farmers, the workers—and a certain portion of the lower stratum of the middle class neither produce nor consume gossip. All the defamatory remarks that the UCN men were tossing about remained on home ground. The slander could not leap over the great wall that separated the middle class from the masses. But I did communicate with the people, and if I repeated the slander to them in order to refute it, I would be acquainting them with it. This could prove to be a boomerang. If I said that the UCN was accusing us of receiving money from a Trujilloist, how many people might be prompted to think it might be true?

Moreover, if a sector of the middle class—probably not the upper stratum—rejected the gossip, that sector would conclude that the Civic Union methods were evil and consequently would reject the UCN. This was possible because gossip, slander, and the lowest kind of attack had been employed by Trujillo's regime. A sector of the middle class, albeit a small one, ought to be disgusted by the resurrection of the "Foro Público" ("Public Forum"), the scurrilous newspaper column defaming those Trujillo had marked for extinction; if there was such a sector, it would drop out of the Civic Union.

It was my opinion, then, that the UCN's attacks on the PRD would eventually boomerang. The best strategy was to let the campaign run its course until that happened.

The campaign did not damage the PRD, but it left the country without a political instrument that could make the revolution. By December, the Balaguer government was the only political instrument that could make a revolution, because it had at its disposal a trained bureaucracy and a devoted Congress, plus the backing of the Armed Forces. During the twelve days of the general strike, the Army had remained stanchly loyal to Balaguer, and Congress had approved every one of the Chief Executive's recommendations with the same rapidity and the same solidarity as in Trujillo's time. This meant that, objectively, Balaguer could effect a revolution. But subjectively, Balaguer could not, because the pressure that he was subjected to compelled him to surrender his power.

One afternoon in December, UCN Secretary General Baquero appeared at Number Seven Polvorín Street, where I was staying as the guest of a sister. He wanted to talk to me. We went across the street to Number Eight, where another sister of mine lived. Upstairs, Baquero said that he wanted to discuss something confidential with me.

He had come in the name of the UCN to ask that the PRD select three men for Dr. Fiallo's Cabinet. At any minute, he said, Balaguer was to designate Fiallo as Minister of the Armed Forces, then resign as President, whereupon, as provided by the Constitution, Fiallo automatically would become President. Baquero said that it was Fiallo's wish, and the Civic Union's as well, that his Cabinet include three members from the PRD and three from the 14th of June, with the UCN to hold the remaining half-dozen seats.

Baquero told me that two UCN leaders, Dr. Jordi Brossa and Fiallo, had visited Balaguer in his home the previous night and had presented him with this solution to the political crisis. Baquero added that the 14th of June leaders were aware of the move and were now deciding whether they would participate in Fiallo's Cabinet.

This all struck me as so infantile that I almost laughed

aloud. I told Baquero that I would convene my party's Executive Committee, but that I personally would oppose PRD participation. This meeting never came off because later that same afternoon Balaguer announced his resignation in a radio address that produced general surprise.

That was the UCN's first public demonstration that they wanted power and would fight to get it. All right, what did they want power for? It was not until September or October, 1962—about a year after the events just related—that the Civic Union offered a government program to the country. UCN participants in the government that succeeded Balaguer's demonstrated that not only had they no idea of how to go about reforming Dominican conditions, but they intended to use their power only for the personal benefit of their high officials.

The revolution, then, was lost. Instead, mobs formed and tracked down any scapegoat, or unearthed Trujillo's victims and dug up martyrs' bones. On the day that Baquero came to my house to urge the PRD to take part in the—in his opinion—inevitable government of Fiallo, I later went to PRD National Headquarters. I rarely visited there; from early morning until late at night, I spent all my time at home receiving people who wanted to see me. Headquarters, facing Columbus Park, was thronged by a perpetual multitude of men and women. The PRD was growing day by day, as were the number of neighborhood and provincial delegates who arrived at Headquarters for instructions, forms for new party members, and membership cards. The place had become such a gathering spot that we could no longer hold Executive Committee meetings there because the number of people would not let us work. But that afternoon, after speaking with Baquero, I went to Headquarters.

Strangely, when I arrived, Columbus Park was deserted. But fifteen minutes later, the park swarmed with three or four hundred people, armed with clubs, pipes, spokes, chains, and stones. They were yelling that one of Trujillo's informers was in PRD Headquarters and that we should turn him over to them so that they could use him to avenge Trujillo's many victims.

I went out on the balcony. I said that if there was an informer on the premises, I personally would turn him over to the police—but not to the mob. "You," I told them, "have no right to take justice into your own hands. If a judge can make mistakes, how can anyone be sure that a mob will not make a mistake?"

I was answered with a general hooting and a deluge of stones thrown at Headquarters. I withdrew inside, from where I could hear the shouts: "Juan Bo is the thug! Juan Bo is the thug! Juan Bo condemns himself!" Had the demonstration been staged to show the public that the PRD was linked with the Trujilloists? Was the timing coincidental, or had my trip to Headquarters been watched? I knew that this could be the beginning of a campaign more violent than rumors, gossip, and slander. But I was not about to give in. Nothing on earth would have made me give in. If by my stand I was gambling the very life of the PRD, my own prestige, and the patient labor of my companions, it did not matter to me. My friend Miolán, who was beside me, did not waver for a moment. Nothing could break us down. I personally telephoned the police. The supposed informer later cleared himself of all charges. He had been a mere chauffeur to Pedrito Trujillo, and neither an informer nor an agent of the political police.

That same afternoon, while stones continued to rain down on Headquarters, I tape-recorded my radio message for that night. I remember that I did not use notes. And what did I talk about? I spoke on the necessity of distributing Trujillo's lands among landless peasant families, at the rate of about 15 acres each. It was the first time I dealt with this subject, which was to be a key issue in the 1962 election campaign.

These were hectic days. A fight for power was being waged in a country that did not know the ground rules for political battles in a democracy. An avalanche of resentment, passions, hatreds, and ambitions tumbled over Dominican soil. The UCN used Fiallo's personal prestige for a shield. Fiallo himself was a pawn being moved about without his having the remotest notion of how the game was going or what part he had in it. When he realized the bad impression produced by his visit to Balaguer's house, and his appeal for Balaguer's resignation in order to have himself named President, he accused his friends of making him a public fool and said that he was going to renounce public life. Morales Carrión, feeling that Fiallo's withdrawal would create a dangerous political gap, managed to dissuade him. Neither Morales Carrión nor the majority of Dominican politicians realized that the National Civic Union had begun its downfall by declaring the December general strike. No matter what happened now, no one could check the UCN's plunge. If Fiallo had stood by his decision to withdraw, he would thereby have become a reserve politician to whom the public could appeal in its time of crisis. But he did not, and probably the Dominican people were better off.

Balaguer agreed to relinquish his position to a team of UCN men, as demanded by the UCN, backed by the U.S. State Department. Washington wanted a collegiate government that had the authority to negotiate, that could accept and comply with loan agreements. This type of government could not be formed without amending the Constitution. So Balaguer appealed to Congress for a constitutional amendment that would create a Council of State—to be made up of seven members, one of whom would be the President—which was to govern until February 27, 1963, and which was to call elections for a Constituent Assembly no later than August 16, 1962, and for President, Congress, and mayoralties no later than December 20, 1962.

The UCN selected four of its members for the Council of State. Someone—no one knows if it was Balaguer, Rodríguez Echavarría, or some other official—chose the two survivors of the May 30 plot. After Balaguer's resignation, one other member was added—a man who had entered the UCN as a 14th of June leader but was no longer a Catorcita.

The procedure for substituting the Council of State for Balaguer had been set up in this way: Balaguer would continue as President of the Republic by serving as President of the Council of State until February 27, 1962. Rafael F. Bonnelly, who was to be President of the Council of State, would be Vice President until Balaguer resigned, at which time he would move to the President's chair.

Thus every necessary move to effect the transfer of power had been outlined, but the UCN was not agreeable to this. It wanted Balaguer out before February 27. The UCN could not wait even a few days; they wanted immediate control. Tension grew by the hour, and finally exploded on January 16, when five persons were killed in Independence Park. Rodríguez Echavarría had sent an armored tank to the park to end the provocations in the UCN local branch, which was there. But instead of dispersing, the UCN mob became aggressive, and the tank crew opened fire. Rodríguez Echavarría lost his head, and amid the commotion produced by this unfortunate episode brought off a lightning *coup d'état*. Balaguer and the other members of the brand-new Council of State were imprisoned in the Palace, although Balaguer was later allowed to leave, and Rodríguez Echavarría immediately formed a three-man junta.

Both Arturo Morales Carrión and John Hill had

left the country shortly before. The following day I received a telephone call from someone who refused to give his name but who was not Dominican. His cryptic words informed me that Hill had arrived and was going to take action immediately. But the caller was so vague that I attached no importance to this. Two days later, however, came the general strike, which ended the coup. That strike culminated seven months of national upheaval, which had begun on July 5 with the arrival of the PRD delegates and which had continued without a single day's let-up until January, 1962.

Still the masses had taken no action. They were simply spectators at a Dominican drama. Their appearance on stage as actors was forbidden by those who claimed to represent their will.

vi

The Social Structure of the
Dominican Republic

Trujillo's death should have brought about some move toward a systematic arrangement of the social order, with the upper stratum of the middle class and part of the middle stratum on one hand, and the rest of the middle stratum, the lower stratum of the middle class, and the masses—workers, farmers, and the unemployed—on the other. It was a little late for a Latin American country to effect such an organization, but this merely demonstrates again how far behind Dominican history lagged.

The upper stratum of the middle class was made up of the more prosperous merchants and professionals, plus landholders, public officials, and some industrialists. Somewhere above these people and occasionally intermingled with them was the "first" caste, a social elite whose ancestry established it in the upper stratum but who lacked the financial means for even the middle stratum. Some upper-stratum families belonged to the "second" level, as did a large part of the middle stratum and almost all of the lower-middle class. At the bottom floundered the rest, the outcasts, the dregs, without any rights.

Trujillo had had every Dominican under his thumb. The name that he had given himself, and that everyone else almost unconsciously had adopted in addressing him or in speaking of him, was "Chief." He had been every Dominican's chief in the broadest sense of the word; he had been Chief just as much to the first-family caste as to the outcasts. Under his leadership, the upper and middle strata of the middle class had grown, and the lower-middle class had also thrived. He had surrounded himself with a small group of industrialists, who had flourished as partners in his enterprises. In the end, Trujillo himself had become the national bourgeoisie. There had been none in the Dominican Republic before he began installing the industries required as the base for his economic empire.

Even today, there is no real bourgeoisie in the country. There are individual industrial magnates, the most prominent of whom are not even Dominicans, but they certainly cannot be regarded as members of a national bourgeoisie. Trujillo's industries became state property after he fell from power, thus making the state the country's greatest industrialist. The social elite and part of the commercial, professional, and landholding upper stratum of the middle class had dreamed of inheriting Trujillo's vast wealth. By acquiring, through political power, his extensive holdings, they could have become the national bourgeoisie.

Therefore, in the wake of Trujillo's death, there was no definition of classes. Nevertheless, the definition should have been produced, not only in economic terms but also in political terms.

Since there are industries, even though there is no Dominican bourgeoisie, there are Dominican workers. Some years ago, even under Trujillo's regime, a working-class consciousness began taking shape, though by 1963 it still was not fully developed. Generally speaking, the same was true of the peasant class, although there is no real peasant-class consciousness. This is the most mobile social group, and it produces a good part of the lower stratum of the middle class and most of the laborers, employed or otherwise, who populate the city slums.

All the underdeveloped countries present comparable sociological pictures, but the countries born of Spain have in their social make-up a historical ingredient that merits careful investigation by sociologists. Traditionally, since the Conquest, Spain, of all the principal European nations, had had the largest social and cultural middle class. But that group lacked the economic resources with which to support itself as a middle class. Although the term "middle class" is modern, it can easily be applied to minor Spanish nobility of the fifteenth to the nineteenth centuries, and even the twentieth. In this grouping were noblemen who were not first-born sons and so had limited inheritances, those who did not belong to the nobility but were involved with it through performance of public functions, and even nuns and priests—all of whom at a moment in Spanish history, made up a large sector of the population.

The economic middle class was made up of people who had come from the lower classes, especially peasants and artisans. But the social and cultural middle class, with pretensions to habits of a superior level, was a social hybrid floating in mid-air without an economic base to support it. And we American peoples inherited from Spain this propensity for a mere shadow of a middle class, because we inherited from the mother country the concepts that gave rise to it. Thus, while in a country with other traditions a poor son of a noble father can establish a business or small industry, in a country with a Spanish heritage this simply is not done. Working is not for the son of a distinguished family. Latin American regions settled by a small colony originating in the Canary Islands have another way of thinking because the Canaries, apparently, made no such distinctions between nobles and plebeians. Thus it came about that in the Baní region of the Dominican Republic, for example, there are no barriers if well-born people want to work.

It is true that underdevelopment maintains societies without social mobility, but it is also true that a great deal of Latin American underdevelopment is in part a direct outgrowth of these static traditions. Many men and women who could have helped change the production methods in these countries did not do so because it would have required them to work, and this would dishonor themselves and their families. Even as the twentieth century dawned, the only vocations open to those who needed to work and whose background obliged them not to were the Army, the priesthood, the professions, and government service. At the end of the last century and the beginning of the present one, the Latin American middle class produced lawyers, doctors, land surveyors, engineers, architects, schoolteachers, priests, nuns, officers, journalists, writers, and a very few people who knew how to produce.

This flaw was intensified in the Dominican Republic. Tyranny became an iron mold in three respects—political, military, and economic. But the former two were merely means of achieving the latter. Trujillo's objective throughout his reign had been to get rich, to become the richest man in the country and possibly one of the richest in the Americas. Necessarily, then, the national area that he held the tightest grip on was the economic. As a consequence, the Dominican Republic could develop only along the lines that Trujillo permitted. It was the Dominicans' misfortune that Trujillo dominated national life in what should have been years of decisive economic, social, and cultural development—years in which the other Latin American nations made the greatest advance, and in which he drastically hampered the Dominicans from developing along the same lines.

The Republic was isolated—not comparatively but absolutely. What the dictatorship permitted to enter the country got in, and what the dictatorship permitted to leave the country got out. News and books, fashions and ideas were imported or exported under equally strict surveillance. The country remained static except in population growth. And this condition aggravated the propensity, inherited from Spain, to produce a cultural and social middle class that could not support itself economically. In short, we had more middle class than we could afford.

The Republic has no reliable statistics, not even for the population. It is estimated that the population ranges between 3,000,000 and 3,500,000. It is also estimated that 70 per cent of the population is rural (for census purposes, those who live in towns of only 1,000 inhabitants are classed as urban even if their sites and means of livelihood are rural). We have no way of determining the number of people in the lower, middle, and upper strata of the middle class. An educated guess would be that the lower stratum seems the most numerous, since the peasantry supplies the largest number of this group, not only in the country but also in the cities. It is also the greatest source of workers in the cities and of the unemployed. The rural middle stratum is far less numerous, but it seems to be the most steady source of the urban middle stratum, because its children generally study and go on to enter this urban social sector. They become professional people or, if not, they acquire tastes and needs that can be sustained only by white-collar or civil-service jobs. Finally, the rural upper stratum is simultaneously urban, as it generally has a city residence, too.

How many Dominicans are there in these middle-class strata?

If they account for 20 per cent of the population, they number around 700,000, of whom more than 300,000 are adult (over eighteen). If they account for 30 per cent, their number exceeds 1,000,000, including more than 400,000 adults.

In any case, the upper stratum probably does not exceed 5,000 families, including about 15,000 adults. And the lower stratum cannot exceed 100,000 families, including about 300,000 adults. The total adult population in the upper and lower strata actually is probably no more than 300,000. The remainder would fall in the middle stratum.

These figures have no statistical basis, but they are not capricious. They are the result of observations made in the field with particular aims and the appreciation of a shopkeeper entering business in a new town and counting his potential customers. Without a working knowledge of the make-up of the Dominican population, more or less accurately estimated, the PRD could never have won the 1962 elections. The entire campaign was based on these calculations—on perfecting our aim to hit the target. Too great an error in either direction would have spelled certain defeat at the polls.

The upper stratum of the middle class has the greatest economic base and thus is the most stable emotionally. In this sense, the lower stratum comes next, although some distance behind as it is always in transit toward the middle stratum, with the result that an appreciable element of the lower stratum has less economic and emotional stability. An important part of the lower stratum is middle stratum in aspirations, culture, and customs, but not in financial resources. Its members float in the social air, and go through life looking for financial opportunity that will support their desires and their social position.

The middle stratum in general is insecure. It embraces most of the country's professions and civil servants, the small businessmen, and those who have no profession but live as though they did. How many can there be—150,000? 200,000? However few, they cannot account for less than 5 per cent of the population. Their ranks include the social elite, especially in towns and cities in the interior. Generally, their lives are arduous. They live where they should not, and want to live where they cannot. Economically, politically, and socially, they are a drag on the Dominican Republic—economically because the country cannot support them, politically because their emotional instability makes them changeable or indifferent, socially because they have no inner coherence and their social aims are ill-defined.

What we classified as the Spanish middle class had a certain coherence at the time of the Conquest—and the colonization. Its members respected certain principles. They were fiercely Catholic. They unreservedly obeyed the King and his representatives. They believed in society and its laws. They loved Spain blindly. They had no visible means of support, but they clung bravely to certain standards.

The Dominican middle class, on the other hand, is like a cloud that changes shape every five minutes. It gathers, then dissolves; is near, then far; fills with rain, unleashes a deluge, and abruptly vanishes over the horizon borne off by the wind.

From the upper stratum, an important number of whom are foreigners, to a large part of the lower stratum, and including most of the middle stratum, people of the Dominican middle class are, above all, at odds with themselves. They have no pride or self-respect. Their either hate the country in which they were born or now live, or they do not know how to love it. A small number of the middle stratum and a greater number in the lower stratum escape that misfortune, but among the upper stratum and the first-family caste, it is virtually impossible to find a Dominican who loves his country.

This widespread lack of patriotism in the Dominican middle class is disheartening and incomprehensible. I, for one, cannot understand how one cannot love one's country, as I cannot understand how one cannot love one's mother. I tell myself that this absence of love for one's country is caused by the insecurity, dissatisfaction, and anguish in which the Dominican middle class exists.

But I do not accept this. Without love, one cannot create anything. Even a hen, considered the most cowardly of domestic animals, will hurl herself like a little feathered fury against anyone who comes too close to her young. Love makes titans of weaklings, heroes of cowards. Love works miracles.

It is painful to hear most middle-class Dominicans speak of their fellow citizens, or comment on a national crisis. For them, the other Dominican is a loafer, a coward, and a thief. At a critical moment in the life of their country, they all wonder—in their homes, on street corners, in the cafés —when "the Americans" are going to do something. They invent news items that "the fleet" is on its way or that "the President" said this or that—referring to the U.S. and not the Dominican President. Throughout the thirty-one years of Trujillo's domination, the majority of the middle class were waiting for the U.S. to throw Trujillo out of power.

With few exceptions, businessmen, professionals, soldiers, priests, journalists, and men and women lack the dignity of patriotism because they lack that stabilizing and creative element called love—love for one's own, for one's country, history, destiny. That last word holds the key to this attitude: The Dominican middle class, lacking a stable present, has no faith in its destiny. It does not believe in its future, and therefore its existence as a social group has no objective. It is submerged in a sea of tribulations.

Because of this attitude, middle-class Dominicans have not yet established a scale of moral values. They feel loyalty to nothing, not to a friend, nor to a party, nor to a principle, nor to an ideal, nor to a government. Their only important value is money because with it they can live on the level that socially and culturally they belong on. To make money, they forget all loyalties.

This spiritual wasteland fortunately excludes a part of the lower and middle strata, which began to react against these conditions around 1959 and 1960. Mostly Catorcitas by membership or inclination, they manifested their reaction in an intense nationalism, which, as already explained, was easily converted into anti-Americanism.

The great popular masses, living within their own economic and social framework, are an entirely different matter. Here, intact, are the national virtues: love of their compatriots, their land, their music, their food; loyalty to friends and party, and to certain simple but generous ideas. This does not mean that all of the masses embody these qualities. In no social sector do the people act as a bloc. As in the middle class there are a number who have reacted against its lack of faith and patriotism, so in the masses there are outcasts, without principles, with no more emotional activity than that experienced by the beasts in eating, sleeping, drinking, reproducing. To support themselves these people take to crime, if necessary. Such a marginal element exists in all human groups and is the source of delinquents.

The Dominican situation is certainly not unique in the Americas, but it has particular aspects that aggravate those characteristics that are common to underdeveloped countries. A similar situation existed in Venezuela, for example, from 1940 to 1950. However, Venezuela had such a strong tradition of patriotic struggle that no Venezuelan social group could entrust the solution of its problems to foreign intervention. All Venezuela underwent its drama with Spartan valor because all the Venezuelans knew that their country had produced exceptional men in the past and believed that it would do so again in the future. In short, Venezuelans had faith in their own destiny.

The Dominican middle class was very small when it lashed out to establish the Republic in 1844. It was still small when it fought Spain in 1863 to restore the Republic. Why has it no faith in its country now?

Perhaps the explanation lies in the fact that throughout the twentieth century to date, the Dominican people have been victimized by national weaknesses of monumental proportions. The century began in the middle of disastrous civil wars, which ceased in 1916 only because of an American military occupation, which lasted eight years. There were six years of peace before, along with the economic crisis of 1929, the dictatorship of Trujillo arrived. The imposition of his regime smothered any hope of change, and submerged the country in an unmerciful system of terror and exploitation. The middle class, more conscious of its situation, began losing faith in its country's future. As this faith declined, so did the capacity to love and to fight.

Only once did three strata of the middle class act in unison—during the strike that toppled the Rodríguez Echavarría junta in January, 1962. But do not forget that behind this was American power. Without the backing of officials representing the U.S. Government, the move might not have been so swift or well-coordinated. True, it was the culmination of seven months of political turmoil, but even so, how would there have been a strike unless its sponsors had faith in their victory because Consul General Hill supported them?

In any case, as has been said, the masses took no part in the strike. By January, 1962, the masses were estranged from the middle class, and in less than two months the social elite was to lose its national prestige in one blow.

The Middle Class in Politics

Even up to the middle of 1961, the country seemed completely unaware that invisible boundaries divided the Dominicans into diverse factions that did not communicate with each other. Pure instinct told the masses that they were lower than other people; they had no notion of who those other people were or why they were up there.

Under Trujillo, the various classes mingled, but people did not move out of the one in which they belonged. Class feeling was never displayed publicly, although it was very much alive in that portion of the upper stratum of the middle class with celebrated names, and among an appreciable part of the middle stratum, especially in the interior of the country. The less income a man had, the stronger his class feeling seemed to be. The greater his financial difficulty in living up to his category, the greater his awareness of his social importance. As a result of this attitude, the first families developed a clan feeling, and any offense by the dictatorship against a cousin, nephew, or brother-in-law was an affront to the entire clan.

If Trujillo conferred power, by means of an important public appointment, on a member of the lower-middle class—as he did on many occasions—that functionary could count on the obedience of any of the elite who might be among his subordinates. They would drink and chat with him at official gatherings, but that was as far as matters would go. Although he might represent all of Trujillo's power, Anselmo Paulino was always Anselmo Paulino, a man of the people, and no illustrious family would sit at his table. Trujillo's iron will was never strong enough to smash these invisible barriers.

When he died, "the kernels of corn began to separate from the ears," as a peasant might say, in an image from his environment. So subtly that it seemed almost natural, the masses began joining the Dominican Revolutionary Party. The upper and middle strata went over to the Civic Union, the leadership of which was from the elite first families. Soon, part of the middle stratum, most of the lower stratum, and almost all of the masses consciously realized the lines of demarcation. For the first time in Dominican history, the people as a whole felt the existence of the barriers that divided them.

Guided by the elite in the upper and middle strata— among the latter were the PSP Communists, to the amazement of Communists in other countries—young and old alike repudiated Joaquín Balaguer as a Trujilloist, and chose for his successor Rafael F. Bonnelly. Because he had become known as an anti-Trujilloist? No. Because he belonged to their class. Rafael F. Bonnelly was just as Trujilloist as Balaguer. Up and down, sideways, frontwards, and backwards, Bonnelly had been as Trujilloist as Balaguer and more responsible than Balaguer for some of the worst aspects of Trujilloism.

Balaguer, who had received a doctor of law degree in Paris, was not Trujillo's lawyer. Bonnelly, who held a law degree from the University of Santo Domingo, was Trujillo's choice to legalize his forcible seizures of land and property. Balaguer, a good orator, delivered many addresses supporting Trujillo. Bonnelly, a reader of speeches, read as many in favor of Trujillo as Balaguer wrote. Balaguer never served Trujillo in posts requiring him to take repressive measures. Bonnelly was for years Minister of the Interior and Police, the instrument of Trujillo's repressive policies. No one can prove that Balaguer got rich from Trujillo's favors; nobody can prove that Bonnelly left Trujillo's service with the same property he had had at the outset of his career as an official of the dictatorship.

The Dominican people, not corrupted by selfish interests, caught on instinctively and rapidly to these class divisions. But middle-class Dominicans became frightened when the PRD began to tackle the country's social problem. The reaction of the middle class—especially the elite and the upper and middle strata—was to accuse us of Trujilloist affiliations, of being allied to Balaguer, because we attacked the social problem instead of attacking the Trujilloists. Fear that the masses would learn the causes of the situation created so much confusion in the middle class that Balaguer himself, as late as October, 1963—that is, after the September coup that overthrew the democratic government of which I was President—accused me of plunging the country into a class war. This was amusingly like the malaria victim who accuses the doctor who has diagnosed the disease of having given it to him. It was the more amusing because Balaguer himself was a principal target of the first families' hatred. As 1964 rolled around, the UCN attacked Balaguer through the pen of a much-honored bard, a university professor who had been Deputy Minister of Education while Balaguer was Minister in Trujillo's Cabinet. This "poet laureate" wrote in an article that Balaguer was an insignificant person due to his humble origins as the son of a Puerto Rican immigrant, and as a boy he had worked in a grocery store. This old subordinate of Balaguer's stirred up the class fight in the Dominican Republic long before I spoke of it. And although the bard failed to mention it, he was doubtless aware of the opposite example: Bonnelly had never had to work, had had entree into the Santiago clubs where distinguished families met, while in that same city young Balaguer was selling penny portions of soap to the neighborhood poor.

What a disgraceful crime to accuse Balaguer of—working in a grocery store! How can Trujillo be forgiven for making him an Ambassador, Minister of Education and Fine Arts, Vice President, and later President of the Republic? One could forgive Trujillo for making the bard an Under Secretary; Bonnelly a Congressman, Senator, Minister of State, and Ambassador; Jacinto B. Peynado and "Pipí" Troncoso de la Concha Presidents of the Republic. These were all men of breeding. But not Joaquín Balaguer, who had been in a humble cradle. Thus a university professor expressed himself in 1964.

That same year another university man, a history professor and daily columnist for one of the capital's two leading newspapers, said openly that he would never again mention my name in his column, in spite of my having been made President by the majority will of the people expressed in elections supervised by the OAS. This history professor is a grandson or great-grandson or some such descendant of a gentleman who was President of the Republic five times during the past century. That gentleman, although sired by the bastard son of a priest, and born of a slave girl, established a very distinguished family, accumulated an enormous fortune, and produced descendants who did not have to work in grocery stores.

Members of the Council of State were chosen to serve in

the government not for their ability or for the fervor of their opposition to the Trujillo regime, but for their social importance. Among the seven Councilors were a priest with the rank of monsignor, three men with family names antedating the wars against Haiti, and one whose famous name dated back to the nineteenth-century dictator De Lilís. Only two had never been Trujilloists, although another two had participated in the plot that cost the tyrant his life. The Cabinet of the Council of State swarmed with personages from the incredible Dominican aristocracy.

All the Councilors of State were UCN men, except for the two who had participated in the plot to assassinate Trujillo, and so was the entire Cabinet. The National Civic Union had launched its drive to capture the government with an avowal that it was patriotic and apolitical, and in a few days thousands of UCN people had taken over official posts, from Embassy positions to minor mayoralties.

During early January, 1962, until about the tenth of the month, the PRD Executive Committee continued to recommend that we participate in the new government. Miolán's argument was that if the UCN occupied all the key posts during a political campaign, it would become the country's dominant political force. My thinking was that the Civic Union would burn itself out in the government. Also, I felt that its converting to a party would kill it, because its vital force was the middle-class youth, principally the Catorcitas, who had in good faith accepted the Civic Union leaders as apolitical patriots and would react violently when they realized that they had been deceived.

While preparing to assume leadership of the government, the UCN launched a campaign to discredit the 14th of June Movement, accusing it of being Communist-inspired. This campaign was conducted everywhere, from pulpits to schools. Doubtless there were Communists in the 14th of June, though perhaps fewer than in the UCN itself.

Nevertheless, the great majority of Catorcitas were not Communists, nor were they inclined to be. They were middle-class young people—some from the upper stratum, the strongest representation from the middle stratum, and others, perhaps the most aggressive ones, from the lower stratum. They were young people who had suddenly appeared in an unpatriotic middle class with an advanced case of nationalism, an impetuous and even wild nationalism, which made them admire Fidel Castro for his nationalist fury, as well as for his exemplification of the guerrilla leader who had toppled a dictator's army.

To accuse these young men and women, 80 per cent of whom were students, of being Communists was tantamount to encouraging them to be Communists. Young people react with emotions, not logic, and Latin American young people have good reason to be resentful. So when they react, they do so unthinkingly, with the desire to destroy anything that hurts them. Thus, if the gentlemen of the UCN so feared the Communists, then the best way to get back at these gentlemen was to lean toward the dreaded enemies.

While the time to take power was still far off and the UCN was still "patriotic and apolitical," it displayed not the slightest concern about the Communist danger. Moreover, the UCN was organized on the basis of a right wing consisting of the upper stratum—with the first-family faction in command—and a democratic, left-wing youth group from the 14th of June. Such a structure was possible because the Catorcitas lent their own secret organization to the gentlemen of the right wing. Catorcita leaders combed every town in the country for new UCN members. And between the right wing and the youthful left wing, there existed a strong tie: an important cell of PSP Communists. These remained in top UCN spots until October, 1962. The UCN used them as links with the Catorcitas. Then, later, the UCN turned on the Catorcitas and accused them of being Communists. The worst of it, as far as the Catorcitas were concerned, was that the charge was made only after the UCN had gained full control of the government.

Certainly, there were Communists in the 14th of June. A few Communist leaders had infiltrated its high command as well as its propaganda office. We in the PRD had suspected that. And our conclusions were confirmed shortly afterward by a purge within the 14th of June that forced out not only the Communists but also a group of moderates. Around the middle of 1962, the 14th of June was an intensely nationalistic organization; its principal leader, Manuel Tavarez Justo, was strongly inclined to the Fidelism of 1959–60, and the majority of members were pro-Fidel and anti-American in leanings, but openly antagonistic toward the PSP Communists and the so-called Marxist-Leninist-Fidelists of the MPD. Until the death of Tavarez Justo and a group of his companions in December, 1963, this antagonism continued, and on several occasions broke out in violence.

Now, for the UCN, the time had come to wage war within their own organization since the 14th of June was part of the Civic Union, so they temporarily shelved their anti-PRD campaign. The PRD had not replied to the UCN's campaign against it. The UCN knew that we were not going to dispute their assuming leadership of the government. We had advised the Council of State that if it approved and was committed to carrying out a government program, we would cooperate, but from the sidelines and without going to public meetings. They need fear no underhanded action from us, no conspiracy. Our position was clear: All we wanted was to create in the masses an awareness of what their problems were and how they could go about solving them through democratic procedures. Knowing our attitude, the National Civic Union could forget about us and concentrate on its forthcoming internal battle.

The 14th of June, even as part of the UCN, following its principles and having its representatives on the UCN high command, preserved its status as an independent organization. The 14th of June, along with a few PSP and MPD members, was the UCN's action group. By November, 1961, however, the public knew of the differences between the UCN and Catorcitas, and in January, 1962, the division was only too clear. When the break came, the Catorcita leaders in the UCN top command deserted the 14th of June and continued their political activity as UCN members.

The split was the immediate consequence of the UCN's transformation from a "patriotic and apolitical" organization into a political party. That change came about after the UCN had already entrenched itself in the Council of State.

What I had written for *Life en Español* in July, 1961, was becoming a reality in January, 1962. The clock of Dominican history, stopped during the thirty-one years of Trujillo's dictatorship, had begun running again, but faster than normal. This was reasonable. After all, the country had a lot of catching up to do, and very little time in which to do it. The break between the UCN and the 14th of June came about early in January, 1962, less than sixty days after the flight of the Trujillos, at which time the UCN and Catorcitas had been firmly united. The clock of Dominican history was indeed running fast.

At this point, what was the position of the masses, and what was the position of the Dominican Revolutionary Party?

Neither the masses nor the PRD nor the 14th of June had anything to do with the formation of the Council of State. The UCN, the U.S. Embassy, General Rodríguez Echavarría, and Balaguer each had a hand in creating it, and the masses and the PRD accepted it without much public comment pro or con. But the people and the PRD had their say in private. In the days during which the Council was being formed, Nicolás Pichardo and Humbertilio Valdez Sánchez came to my house late one night and awakened me. Valdez Sánchez, a member of the PRD Executive Committee, explained that he had brought Pichardo because the men selecting the Council of State had insisted on consulting the PRD about their desire to put Valdez Sánchez on the Council. He had said he could not accept, but they wanted to have this confirmed. I told Pichardo that the PRD had decided not to participate in the UCN's government—which must have come as a relief to his companions, as it meant there were more posts to go around for them.

We in the PRD stuck to our task of developing political awareness among the masses. We encountered great obstacles, but we were making progress. While the UCN was taking power—without opposition from us—the men and women already established throughout the country as PRD leaders were devoting themselves to setting up committees in rural areas and urban neighborhoods, in municipalities and provinces. As passionately dedicated as Crusaders, they worked day and night making converts, circulating pamphlets, gathering desks and typewriters and chairs and everything else necessary to set up party offices here and there. They spoke on the radio and organized rallies; they obtained medicine and clothing and distributed it among the people in the slums; they assisted everywhere there was a community need, doing whatever they could to alleviate it, resolving conflicts between management and labor or citizens and authorities. The Dominican Revolutionary Party was being built by the people. And it was led by a few dozen men and women who found that it voiced their concerns and expressed the necessity to build a better

Dominican Republic, with more justice, less hunger, and an end to evil traditions.

In all truth, the people joined the party in greater numbers than even we had expected. After the Council of State was established, people almost threw themselves at the PRD. Almost as quickly as it takes to tell, the masses—who had been anti-UCN to begin with but who were more so after the general strike in December, 1961—realized that by converting from a "patriotic and apolitical" group to a political party, the UCN had exposed its deception. The reason for saying it was not a political party was simply to gain power more easily. The masses feared anyone who was out for power. Trujillo had been the epitome, in their thinking, of a man who had wanted power, and in order to get it and keep it would stop at neither bloodshed, land grabbing, nor destroying anyone who stood in his way. The UCN had declared a holy war on the Trujilloists, but had never mentioned the people's problems. Now, suddenly, there was the UCN, sitting on Trujillo's throne. *What was it doing there?* The people watched, listened, and grew silent; then they ran to join the PRD.

Early in February—around the ninth or tenth—I left on a trip to Venezuela. I had a round-trip ticket to Curaçao. But I had not one cent for the passage south from Curaçao. I had to go to Lima, to take part in a Conference for Democracy and Liberty. An American friend I had known since 1945 lent me $100. As the plane flew from Santo Domingo south across the Caribbean toward Curaçao, young people in the capital started their onslaught on UCN locals. General Rodríguez Echavarría, who had been under arrest since mid-January, had secretly embarked in the night for Puerto Rico, and young Catorcitas seized on this as an excuse for a wild demonstration against the UCN's conduct. The conversion to a party in order to take power, after falsely claiming to be patriotic and apolitical and thereby gaining the services of the best Dominicans, and then accusing those same Dominicans of being Communists, only proved that the UCN was using Trujillo's old tactic—calling anyone he wanted eliminated a Communist.

The UCN officially declared that before leaving for Venezuela, I had organized these riots. The purpose of this lie was easily divined: The UCN now recognized that the Dominican Revolutionary Party was the only real enemy it had to fear. Someone had indiscreetly let the UCN know that in January alone PRD membership had grown by more than 70,000—an average of 2,000 a day every day, including Saturdays and Sundays.

The New Language

Bribes of villas and castles were believed, in many Latin American political circles, to have won the 1962 elections for the PRD. This idea was spread by U.S. newsmen who had not heard a single one of my speeches. They had picked up most of their material from people of the upper and middle strata of the middle class who frequented the few good Santo Domingo hotels, or from U.S. businessmen known to favor the National Civic Union.

The UCN high command fed on rumors and gossip and spewed forth more of the same. Before Trujillo, Dominican political campaigns depended heavily on the lofty device of telling Joe Blow that John Doe, leader of the other party, had said a few nasty things about him. Thus Joe Blow would easily become Doe's enemy. In the nineteenth century, the political philosopher and reformer Eugenio María de Hostos had been right in saying that Dominican politics consisted of petty gossip-mongering elevated to the level of affairs of state. In the twentieth century, Trujillo increased the importance of gossip on the national political

77

scene even more. Gossip, because of its deceitful nature, always held the seed of a slander, and Trujillo made slander the customary weapon in a political fight. Traditionally, then, everything political was thought of in terms of persons: Tom is this, Dick is that.

The PRD brought a completely new approach to Dominican politics. National problems, not individual persons, were what the PRD talked about, along with ways to solve these problems, rather than one man's vices or virtues. The PRD was always oriented toward a specific audience, and that was the common people. For the first time, the masses were the object of someone's attention, and this quickly gave them a feeling of importance. Someone endowed them with social significance, and that someone was the PRD. Logically, they joined our party.

A friend of mine tells this story: In the days when the UCN was a "patriotic and apolitical" organization and not a political party, he was in a store when a young man entered. This young man, who was clearly from an upper-class family, had some papers in his hand. He explained that they were UCN membership forms and he was taking applications. The shopkeeper signed, his son signed, the clerk signed. At this point, the fellow who swept the shop and ran errands asked to be included.

"No, not you," said the UCN recruiter. "We have enough members now with these others."

For that young man, as for the Civic Union leaders, a man of the people like the sweeper was unimportant and, therefore, not worth signing up as a member.

For the PRD, on the other hand, the important ones were the men and women of the people. We wanted to be not a party of distinguished people, but rather a party of the great popular masses. And from the very first, we went after them. It would have been foolish to try to win over the people by offering them things; there was not enough money in the world to give each of them what he needed. But it was not foolish to convince them that they had the right to be given the opportunity to obtain what they needed. There is an enormous difference between offering a man a refrigerator and instilling in him an awareness of his *right* to own a refrigerator; and before the Dominican people heard the voice of the PRD, they thought they had no right to own a refrigerator because it was meant for only a chosen few.

One night I heard Dr. Fiallo say at a press conference that he had never offered "electric iceboxes" to farmers "as another leader has." He was referring to me. I never offered iceboxes. The only thing I offered during the entire campaign was the assurance that if the PRD came to power, land would go to the landless. Fiallo told the same press conference that he had gone to Samaná and had spoken there of the coconut industry, but that he had not offered the people of Samaná the Columbus Lighthouse. The Columbus Lighthouse was an idea that a group of government people had gotten into their heads before Trujillo's time and that Trujillo had hoped to bring about. It was supposed to be a monument to the explorer, a splendid construction to be put up on the outskirts of Santo Domingo at a cost of several million dollars, to be contributed by all the American nations. At the beginning of 1962, when the Punta del Este Conference met in Uruguay to lay the basis for the Alliance for Progress, Fiallo sent the Dominican delegation a cable suggesting that they request the allocation of necessary funds—for the country's development? for the improvement of schools? to promote agriculture? No. To erect the Columbus Lighthouse.

From the time the UCN high command learned, toward the end of January, 1962, that the PRD membership was close to 200,000, Civic Union propaganda organs hammered away day after day at Miolán and me, speculating whether I was this or that, whether Miolán had done this or that; the most incredible gossip and slander circulated over the UCN telephone network. Yet the PRD continued to grow. When Fiallo was asked the size of the UCN's membership on a *Meet the Press* program, he stated that there were 600,000. Why did he say such a thing? Because the PRD had applied to the Central Electoral Board for official certification, and had offered proof of 300,000 members. The PRD was the first party to apply for certification. The UCN was certified only after its government—the Council of State—adopted legislation dropping the requirement for a party to disclose the size of its membership in order to be certified. Still, Fiallo had said that the UCN had 600,000 members. We the PRD leaders knew that ours was the country's largest party. We also knew that in April, when Fiallo made his statement, no Dominican party could claim such a huge membership because more than half the voters were still uncommitted. The total electorate—which was divided among the PRD, the 14th of June, and the UCN—could not possibly have amounted to more than 1,200,000.

Nevertheless, the PRD did not bother to contradict statements like that. *Democratic Tribune,* the PRD's midday radio program, aired the people's daily problems, union claims, the lack of electricity in communities, an unjust arrest by the police, what qualifications a given public office required, etc. During a fifteen-minute segment of the program, I gave the party's views on matters of general public interest.

The UCN distorted what I said, either because they failed to listen or because they wanted to confuse the public. I myself heard several UCN people admit that they had failed to listen because they had not wanted to be convinced; thus it is possible that they did not hear the program and relied upon gossip and irresponsible reports. One day, for example, an article in the UCN paper attributed to me the foolish statement that under a PRD government, maids and cooks would earn 60 pesos ($60 in U.S. currency) per month. In the entire Dominican Republic, there are probably not 10,000 homes with maids or cooks, and in all of these, or at least a good number of them, the lady of the house would call down a plague on my soul if such a wage increase was guaranteed. In fact, there probably are 100,000 women in the country who would be delighted to work as maids or cooks, and if these ladies all heard the UCN say I would guarantee them 60 pesos per month, they would join the PRD. In those days, the pay for a maid or cook was from 5 to 15 pesos a month, more often the former than the latter. The difference between this and 60 pesos was, from a voter's point of view, not to be scoffed at.

By failing to understand the masses or their psychology or their language, the UCN was actually making propaganda for the PRD. Convinced that the people were incapable of judgment, intelligence, or concern for the truth, the UCN addressed only "important" circles of nationals and foreigners, and continued commenting on what they said the PRD said. U.S. correspondents, who in neither the Dominican Republic nor any other spot in Latin America look for their information in places where there is no whisky or telephones, cabled in dispatches painting that false version of the PRD campaign. Because of them and because of many diplomats with the same limitations, governments and political circles throughout Latin America believed that the PRD—and especially myself—were conducting a scandalously demagogic campaign.

I have lived in many Latin American countries and have been witness to several political campaigns. In all seriousness, I can state with assurance that none has ever been so scrupulous or responsible as that of the PRD in 1962. The task undertaken by the PRD—to create an awareness of the country's problems—is unparalleled in Latin America. Unparalleled because it made the people understand thoroughly in less than a year and a half of speaking day after day in the people's own language, clearly and simply. Unparalleled because things were said that had never before been said to the great masses. Unparalleled because we accomplished it so cleverly that not even the shrewdest members of the upper and middle strata of the middle class were aware of the extent of its completeness. Our only precedent was the Popular Democratic Party's campaign in Puerto Rico in 1938–40, but the conditions of the Puerto Rican masses at that time could not be compared to those of the Dominicans in terms of their ignorance, their neglect, and the gravity of their problems. We had to work much harder than Luis Muñoz Marín's PPD in order to get across each of these problems and its possible solution, and to give the masses some concept of what a modern democracy is and how it functions.

There is a peculiarity about communicating in the Dominican Republic. It exists even though our country has no racial or cultural minorities, unlike other Latin American nations whose Indians have different languages and customs. The Dominican masses interpret many words in their own way, so that it is almost as if the masses have one language and the middle class another, even though they use the same words. The only difference is in the meaning, occasionally the pronunciation, and very frequently the combination of words and their order in the sentence, which necessarily involves, of course, a special syntax. I was born into the lower stratum of the middle class, very close to the masses. As a child, I lived many years in the country around La Vega, and I learned to express myself in the people's patois. In the region where I was born, the farmers and many of the townspeople speak practically a dialect. It is not important whether one speaks to these people like a person of pure Cibao stock, so long as one can make oneself understood by using syntax that adequately encompasses both the concept and the connotation of the words in the sense that these people give them. As these things are generally the same for the masses all over the country, although the people in the Cibao area might have their own pronunciation, it was possible to find a way of speaking that would be clearly understood by the popular mind in Cibao and other areas.

And I knew how. As a child, perhaps drawn to it by my then unknown but undoubtedly existent vocation of writing, I instinctively was a careful observer of the people around me, of their reactions, and I was able to evolve a fairly sound notion of their mental processes, their aspirations, and their worries. The psychological world of the common people was distinct from that of the middle class. Between the rural peasant and the urban poor and unemployed, there was a strong affinity, because the poor and the unemployed had come from the countryside. Between the peasant and the lower stratum of the middle class, there was also an affinity, but not in aspirations or worries, because the lower stratum, which was principally of farm origin—although lately it has also derived from laborers and even the urban poor and jobless—aspired to enter the middle stratum and took for itself the concerns of the middle stratum. But the middle and the upper strata had practically no relationship with the peasants and the workers and the unemployed. One group did not understand the other, and even though both spoke the same language, they were not saying the same thing.

In order to illustrate for the PRD youth how they should express themselves before the masses, I used the example of an upper-stratum gentleman, from one of the first families, who was laden with academic degrees. In his radio oratory he repeatedly used the expression, "That entails a betrayal of revolutionary ethics." I pointed out to them that for the people, the word for "entails" ("*entraña*") meant the entrails of animals, what they themselves would call "guts." And the word "ethics" meant nothing at all to most of the people; if somebody did understand the word, it would only connote a consumptive, because that was the colloquial interpretation. The sentence, then, had no meaning at all for the people; it might as well have been Arabic.

Speaking words comprehensible to the masses also meant speaking to the middle class if one picked one's words carefully, but if one could not find a middle way, then one had to speak in the language of the people. Even using that language, progress was slow. It was necessary to make clear to the people little by little everything that could and should be important to them. One had to speak to them each day on one theme, one subject, exhausting it completely, and if there was not enough time to exhaust it, one would continue with that theme one or even two days more if necessary.

Many of my radio chats were improvised, others were given from notes, but few were written in advance. This material has been almost entirely lost, and all that remains are a few highlights from the newspapers that published résumés. If anyone would take the trouble to read those résumés, he would see that we never made promises to give anything to anyone, except land and the means to make it productive for the peasants, which was the foundation of the agrarian reform that every Latin American nation must sooner or later effect. Thus, the claim that "Juan Bosch offered too much, and failed to deliver," with which certain political circles in North and South America want to justify the coup of September 25, 1963, plays fast and loose with the truth. The coup was organized before I took over as President of the Republic, and originated in causes a little more complex than that of "offering and failing to deliver." Furthermore, the masses, who voted for the PRD, neither participated directly or indirectly in the coup nor had anything to do with organizing it or carrying it out. Thus, whether or not I had offered and failed to deliver did not cause the coup.

What did I talk about during those days?

Fundamentally, three things: What is a democracy, and how does it function? What are the economic problems of the Dominican Republic? How was Dominican society organized?

In speaking of democracy, I explained what a constitution is and what laws are, how the separate powers of a government function and are interrelated, how and why people vote, and what a political party is. In speaking of economic problems, I explained such abstruse points as what a balance of payments is, what foreign exchange is, what a bank is, why we must produce more and how to go about it, and the difference between foreign and domestic markets. When I spoke on the organization of Dominican society, I explained why the masses were, and always had been, subjugated by a minority. When I mentioned the word minority, I qualified it with the adjective *tutumpote*, a sonorous Dominican colloquialism meaning "big shot." It immediately became popular and it spread through the country and even beyond our borders.

That word had been part of the Cibao country vocabulary when I was a boy. But it had so disappeared from use that in 1961 only old people could remember it. It is difficult to trace its origin. It may perhaps be derived from Latin, the Vulgar Latin of the people, because it seems to sound in that language very much like what it meant to the Dominicans in Cibao around 1912—"*todopoderoso*," an all-powerful gentleman, with an abundance of money. It might have its roots in the years of Haitian occupation; the Haitian dialect has many sounds like *tuntún* or *tutún*. In parts of Spain, *"pote"* meant "in abundance," and an added *"a"* or *"al"* meant "a great deal of."

When I returned to the Republic in October, 1961, the word "bourgeois" was widely used, in its Marxist connotations. This tag was hung on the rich Trujilloists by the youth action group of the Civic Union and the few members of the PSP and MPD. The term could not be applied accurately in the Dominican Republic because there was no creole bourgeoisie. There was an upper middle class engaged in trade, landholding, and even industry, to some extent. But there was no bourgeoisie. I had to invent a word to encompass the elite circles, even though they included men who possessed neither impressive bank accounts nor high public office nor great landholdings nor big businesses. The word had to sound attractive to the masses, be catchy, and be sufficiently self-explanatory to eliminate the necessity of my explaining to the people each day who their traditional exploiters were. No word was more suitable than *tutumpote*. I revived it, and I had used it no more than five times before the people had it on their lips and used it as a weapon in the struggle.

Dominican *tutumpotes* and a few non-*tutumpote* leaders accused me of plunging the country into a class struggle. The class struggle and hatred between classes had always existed in Santo Domingo, only now the first families no longer flaunted it and the people who suffered did not pay attention to it or feel that they should resign themselves to endure injustice. In the early days of Spanish colonization, working-class Spaniards were highly aware of their situation, and anyone who reads Dominican history will learn that peasants, artisans, and soldiers rebelled several times against oppression by Columbus and his family. About the class struggle according to Marxist philosophy—that is, the hatred of the worker for his employer—I said nothing in the political campaign, because, among other reasons, there is no genuine bourgeoisie in the country.

Several times the UCN claimed that I had aroused racial hatred in Santo Domingo. They did not hear what I actually said but listened to rumors and gossip, with the result that one day Fiallo, when he was already the UCN's presidential candidate, said at an appearance that it was untrue that he hated Negroes, that the Negroes were this and that. Once again, as so often in the past, the Civic Union leader was making propaganda for us. The following day I reminded Fiallo that in the Dominican Republic there should be neither whites nor blacks, but only Dominicans.

It was the only time during the entire campaign that I referred to the racial question. I had never touched on it before, nor did I ever deal with it again. I had never had the least bit of racism, neither white nor black. In the Dominican Republic racial discrimination was virtually unknown, in comparison with other countries. If such discrimination had existed, I would have denounced it, at the risk of being accused of demagoguery. There were social divisions, and I had brought them out into the open. I showed them to the people; I said that they were unjust and the source of injustice. It was my duty to do so for the benefit of the great bulk of the Dominican population and for the nation. It is impossible to construct and maintain a republic of free men and women on a foundation of injustice, exploitation, ignorance, and mistreatment.

After the 1962 campaign, the people knew who, in truth, were their enemies and where they were lurking. The people learned to distinguish between a poor devil who earned 70 pesos a month as an informer, and a grand gentleman who wrung enormous fortunes out of a regime backed by informers. And they learned, too, that between the thug and the *tutumpote,* their real enemy was the latter.

By teaching the people this much, I am sure, I have performed a labor of public benefit, and I am proud of it, whatever my adversaries may have to say about it.

ix

Politics and Conspiracy

The 1962 election campaign was finished in April, as far as the PRD was concerned. Our task had been made easier by a few major errors committed by the UCN.

During my South American trip, from February to April 8, the UCN newspaper and radio station hurled forth every lie and insult that Trujillo over the years had used against me. But the Civic Union made the mistake of telling the people, day after day, that I would not come back, that I had abandoned the country, that Ramfis had given me a million pesos so that I would go away. Thus, a trip of limited political significance was converted by the UCN into a decisive event for them.

The public was accustomed to believing that I told the truth, that I was the only one who did. For the masses, telling the truth did not consist of insults or persistent references to Trujillo. For the masses, telling the truth was saying things in such a manner that they would understand them, and above all, teaching them how these things related to them and to their country. My quarter-hour radio program, during which I spoke in the name of the PRD, had become a classroom attended by all the people, a school that led them to discover previously unthought-of facets of their own lives. For them, this was the truth. The people missed the language of truth while I was on my trip, and the UCN made the mistake of announcing that it was gone forever, thus making it the more desirable.

Angel Miolán realized this and acted accordingly. He was skillful in using the masses to show the party's power.

I landed on April 8 at Punta Caucedo Airport, in Santo Domingo, several hours behind schedule, very disturbed by the plane's noise and without imagining what lay ahead. The airport was closed to people. Here and there, though, appeared posters of welcome, among them some with the words "We shall pass, my friend!" The people had learned to use UCN slogans to their author's disadvantage. In the speech in which he announced to the country the UCN's change in status from its previous position of "apolitical patriotism," Fiallo had stated that if the public's esteem for him were placed on one side of a balance scale, and that for all the leaders of all the other parties were put together on another, his side would greatly outweigh the other. He ended his statement with the old rallying cry: "They shall not pass." This, from the lips of the leader of the party in power, proclaimed a will to rule that fell with ill grace on the ears of the Dominican people. The simple, heroic phrase spoken by General Pétain had buoyed the Parisians' spirits as German troops were advancing toward Paris. It was inspiring on the lips of the weak as they turned to face the strong. But used by the strong, already invested with power, to the humblest of their constituents, it only aroused the people to answer: "We shall pass." And we passed.

From the airport, we headed for the city. On the way, thousands of men and women in hundreds of vehicles screamed our party's slogans. By the time we reached town, the throng was multitudinous. We drove through poor neighborhoods, and men, women, and children dashed out into the streets in their nightclothes, shouting until they were hoarse, and ran beside the cars and trucks. "Has everyone gone mad?" I asked, turning to Miolán, who stood beside me in the open convertible. Miolán did not answer; he only smiled.

We drove along a street in the center of the city, and a pretty young girl about twenty years old, if that, screamed "Thief!" at me as I rode by. Was she Catorcita or UCN? Why had she called me a thief? Whom had I ever robbed in my life? Yet I knew where that word had come from. A few days before, in Caracas, I had heard the story from a Dominican industrialist who made his home in the Venezuelan capital and who had made a trip to Santo Domingo for the express purpose of meeting Fiallo, of whom he had been an apostle. On his first and only meeting with Fiallo, the UCN leader had ranted to him about the millions I had made in Venezuela. This industrialist knew me well and knew how I had lived and on what during my exile in Caracas. When that girl yelled "Thief!" from the door of her house, I knew that no one would defeat the Dominican Revolutionary Party. I knew that because this kind of campaign by personal vilification, cut from Trujillo's own pattern, no longer could be considered valid in a country with problems of the masses. Our Republic had greatly changed, for better or worse, under Trujillo, and political tactics effective in 1924 were worthless in the Dominican Republic of 1962. A slanderous charge was no longer any match for a specific accusation supported by facts. That girl, evidently from the middle class, could believe anything she wanted, anything that appealed to her personal taste. But the great mass of people wanted to believe in other things, in a future with justice, in a future without favoritism, in a better tomorrow. And it would be the great mass that would be called on to decide, if an election was finally held.

Elections for a Revisory Constituent Assembly were to be held before August 16, 1962. No preparations had been made for this. Control of the UCN National District Committee—the most important party committee since more than 160,000 voters were concentrated in the District, which embraced the capital—was in the hands of PSP men, and the Civic Union feared that the PRD would denounce this Communist stronghold in their midst. We knew that as long as the UCN made no move to remedy this situation, no elections would take place. But for the PRD and for the country as a whole, it was very important for elections to be held—first, because they would give the people practice in a free election; second, because they would give each party the opportunity of measuring its strength; and third, because only by such a procedure would it be possible to subject the Council of State to a constitutional law that would prevent the violence and deportations that were already going on.

It became my responsibility to conduct a campaign on behalf of elections for constitutional reform, and it was a single-handed undertaking. Not one of the other parties was interested in it. By then, around the middle of 1962, other parties than the PRD, UCN, and 14th of June were functioning, among them the Revolutionary Social Christian Party (Partido Revolucionario Social Cristiano) and a small but very active group called the Nationalist Revolutionary Party (Partido Nacionalista Revolucionario), which was closely allied with the 14th of June.

In Santo Domingo exists what is called a *ventorrillo,* a poor shop or tavern—the most primitive kind of permanent store known to the world of business. It consists of a small window in hut or hovel in the country or in a poor district with a board laid over the sill. On this board, fruits, candles, boxes of matches, candies, and centavo portions of salt or sugar are displayed for sale. A *ventorrillo* can be set up with only a 10-peso investment, and because the neighborhood poor often need a little credit to tide them over, can be sustained with a capital of 50 pesos.

In 1962 the country swarmed with "political *ventorrillos*." A few men aspiring to prominence—seeing their names in the paper and calling themselves party presidents, and of course having a poster with which to negotiate for positions, collect money, and perhaps someday become ambassadors—began setting up political parties. In truth, however, there were only four parties that deserved the name, and of those the largest in membership was the PRD, followed in terms of electoral strength by the UCN. In the opinion of the PRD leaders, the 14th of June could count on more sympathizers than the UCN, but fewer voters, because at least half the Catorcitas were under eighteen years of age. The Revolutionary Social Christians were in a similar situation, though on a smaller scale.

The campaign for elections to revise the Constitution aroused the suspicions of the members of the Council of State. On one occasion, I had mentioned that the Council would enjoy a short life—constitutionally, its term was set at one year—and the UCN, accustomed as it was to distorting my every word, declared that I had predicted the Council's immediate downfall. With the peculiar mentality born of Trujilloism, the Council's President, Rafael Bonnelly, attributed to me his own qualities, accusing me of engaging in conspiracy rather than political leadership, of being power hungry rather than the head of a political party intended to lead the masses toward a political goal. All during this time, I was staying at a friend's farm, not far from Punta Caucedo Airport. One Sunday afternoon, two Army colonels dropped by to visit my friend. Naturally enough, we all chatted a bit. An hour later the 14th of June announced over the radio that I was involved in a conspiracy, that high officers of the Armed Forces had met with me in secret conferences "in the home of a dangerous Trujilloist." Beginning the following day, I was under constant surveillance. The agent to whom fell the first shift of the day wore dark glasses to be discreet and thereby called everyone's attention to himself. If I remember correctly, his name was Zarzuela.

I mention these details of apparently insignificant episodes in order to depict the state of mind of the men directing the country's destiny, and to serve as a basis for explaining what was to happen a year and three months later. Men in government, the UCN and the 14th of June, and many other men besides, had minds geared for conspiracy and not for political struggle. The founding of a democratic society requires a different attitude. Also, there is only one genuine basis for a democratic system: recognition of the fact that the will of the people is sacred, that from it springs the only valid claim to authority. Once started on the road to conspiracy, one can return to a state of justice only through conspiracy. A political leader, a true leader, will not enter into a plot while a door remains open for winning the popular will by legal methods. I was a political leader, but government officials and other PRD adversaries were not willing to accept this fact. Months before, I had been offered an arrangement whereby I could have come to power as the Council of State subsequently had, and I had refused. I had said several times that the PRD would accept power only from the hands of the voters. Neither government officials nor the UCN nor the Catorcitas had heard these words. But if they had, they would not have believed them. As it happens, a political leader—leader, not charlatan—does not say he will do what he is not going to do. Politics is a function of service, and is therefore eminently moral. Because of the climate of cheating, double dealing, and unprincipled behavior that was habitual with the majority of the middle class, the government officials and UCN leaders thought that I had an ulterior motive in so vigorously demanding compliance with the constitutional mandate concerning elections for a Revisory Constituent Assembly—they thought I used this demand as a means of stirring up agitation that would justify a military take-over.

They thought like this because they regarded military coups as a part of politics. Bonnelly had been an important figure in Rodríguez Echavarría's uprising in November, 1961, and he and his colleagues had come to power by means of a back-room agreement, without taking into consideration the will of the people. For this sort of men, the common people were of no consequence. If they needed the pretext of popular backing, they simply agitated it. This the UCN had done. But when it came to making decisions affecting the lives of the people, they were left outside the back room where the decisions were made. In establishing the Council of State, neither other political parties nor labor groups nor cultural organizations were consulted. The UCN high command, Balaguer, Rodríguez Echavarría, and the U.S. Embassy simply went behind closed doors and together drew up the Council. The PRD was asked only to authorize Valdez Sánchez to be a member of the Council of State. This the PRD refused to do. But nothing was said about the Council of State itself, about what it would be, what it would do, who would sit on it.

The government's plan was to seize me some dark night, deposit me at the airport, which was only a few hundred yards from the house in which I was staying, and send me out of the country on the charge that I was a Communist. It was July, 1962. It was thought that my supposed Communist leanings would serve as the necessary excuse for doing away with the PRD. A few military leaders were approached, but they would have nothing to do with the plot. There was another problem: How could the government justify my projected exile to my friends all over the Americas? These people were fully aware that I was not a Communist, that I did not now have, nor had I ever had, any link with the Communist Party. What would they say to Rómulo Betancourt, José Figueres, Luis Muñoz Marín?

The Catorcitas accused me of plotting because they were still obsessed with the past. The ghost of Trujillo left them no peace. Up to a point their attitude was justified. Trujilloism had not been wiped out of either the government or the Armed Forces. But in my case, they were acting under the influence of two different propaganda attacks that, although contradictory, agreed on one point: the necessity of destroying the PRD. One propaganda attack was based on the Communist-inspired tale—the only piece of propaganda allowed into the country by Trujillo—in which Miolán and I appeared as the most despicable political adventurers and, moreover, I was pictured as the State Department's protégé, groomed by it to succeed Trujillo and continue the Dominican dictatorship in Washington's service. I was reminded of the headlines in *Liberación,* a small newspaper printed on lightweight paper that Dominican Communists in exile published in Guatemala and sent into the Republic by clandestine means. I got the feeling of reading once again the wild statements about me that had been printed in *Liberación.* I was reminded also of more recent publications, especially those put out by the Communists in Venezuela, which charged that I was the choice of Betancourt, Washington, and Balaguer to head the new dictatorship, the neo-Trujilloism. The second propaganda attack, originated by the UCN, depicted us as agents of both Ramfis and Balaguer. Thus, for the 14th of

June, the most casual of talks between the military and myself were taken as proof beyond any doubt that I was up to my neck in a Trujilloist conspiracy backed by the United States.

When the course of events was seen more clearly, and it became evident to the whole world that the PRD were neither Washington's agents nor Trujillo's partners nor conspirators nor the accomplices of military adventurers, then the Catorcitas changed their attitude toward us. But the Councilors of State and the Civic Union and the self-appointed leaders of the political *ventorrillos* continued thinking as they had thought in July of 1962, and acted accordingly. The result was the *coup d'état* of 1963.

Elections for a Revisory Constituent Assembly failed to take place, but some reforms were made, thanks to agreements among the Social Christians, the UCN, and the PRD. The UCN had managed to retrieve a difficult situation. Some months later, the PSP Communists who controlled the UCN National District Committee left the organization.

Meanwhile, the PRD was gaining more and more people from the lower-middle class. Our strategy for recruiting members was this: We would go out after the masses, and when they joined the party, they would pull in with them a sizable part of the lower stratum of the middle class. And in the wake of the latter would come a few of the middle stratum. With the utmost care, as if carrying out battle plans or executing a work of art, we developed tactics that implemented our strategy. And perhaps it bears repeating that all of this was brought off without demagoguery, with dignified political conduct. Personally, I found it easier to say No than Yes to any request, but when I undertook a task I carried it out.

Party leaders throughout the country were fully aware of the extent to which they could count on me. They could see me any time. They would not have to listen to any gossip. They would be permitted no backbiting among themselves, and if any internal disagreements arose, they would be expected to resolve them. They could expect no favoritism from me on behalf of any one of them. My role as President of the party—and therefore spokesman for all its members—precluded my giving any direct or indirect support to any intraparty factions or trends. Angel Miolán was Secretary General and therefore chief of the Executive Committee. His responsibility was to put into effect any proposals upon which the Committee had agreed. His position, therefore, required the respect of every PRD member, without exception. We all had our duties carefully outlined, and had to fulfill them. The party would be whatever its members wanted it to be; each one shared the burden of helping it grow spiritually and achieve a disciplined maturity. I knew that while the masses predominated in the party, it would respond to the goals that we had outlined. However, I feared that if the party acquired a middle-class majority, and especially if they occupied top positions, the weakness of that social factor would be reflected in the party as a whole. It was for that reason that our policy regarding memberships concentrated on the masses, with less attention to the lower stratum of the middle class, and very little to the middle stratum.

The party could identify with either the image of the country as it was or the country as it ought to be. In order to project the latter, we needed tools and persons of the highest political integrity. We needed top-level leaders with a strong cultural background and with solid experience in solving social problems. We needed to establish libraries and publish periodicals. It was an important undertaking, and, in it we had the help of Sacha Volman, an extraordinary person of whom I shall speak a little later.

But mobilizing the masses for an election scheduled for

August was a task of incredible proportions. An avalanche of work descended on us, the party leaders, and took up our every waking hour. We trekked from town to town, spoke over the radio, held frequent meetings in order to reach agreements on political events. We had to see leaders from the country, the wards, the towns, the provinces all over the Republic. We had to raise funds, make visits, accept invitations, talk to local and foreign press, and answer letters which poured in at the rate of thousands a month.

The Civic Union, with remarkable persistence, employed all kinds of tricks to confuse the public as much as possible. It spread the notion that I was a mere storyteller, a fabricator of tales. In the common people's language, this implies a man who deceives, who lies. But it happens that I *am* a storyteller. I gained a reputation throughout the Americas as a fiction writer, and I have five published volumes of short stories to my credit. So, instead of respecting what should have been a credit to the nation —literary works belong, after all, to the people and not to their authors—the UCN used my work to mislead the masses.

It had become my fate, because of the timing of history and no other reason, to be the first Dominican writer of the twentieth century to deal with national themes by using characters drawn from the common people. The characters in my stories were farmers, workers, peasants. Everything I was saying during the election campaign of 1962 had already appeared in my first book, *Camino Real (Royal Road)*, published in 1933. In fact, the title story could just as well have been written in 1962.

During this period the Rotary Club—or was it the Lions?—invited me to give a talk on the art of short-story writing. It was the first time I had had the opportunity of speaking before a middle- and upper-stratum audience, and it is one of life's ironies that I spoke on literary matters before cultured people, whereas I spoke on economic, sociological, and political matters before the masses.

I used that lecture the following day in explaining to the people what the word storyteller meant in my case. I told them about the stories that I had written and why I had written them. And so it came about that the Dominican people learned the difference between one who writes tales and one who lives by them.

X
___

A Political School

I do not remember whether it was in June or July that I met U.S. Ambassador John Bartlow Martin. He was a man with a hard face and a good heart, and the mind of a Kennedy liberal, in spite of being a good deal older than President Kennedy. He had been in Adlai Stevenson's circle and had then moved over to Kennedy's camp. He was one of a group of U.S. intellectuals of the democratic left who passionately believed that it was a necessity, a duty, for the United States to lead the world in a crusade to bring the concept of constructive democracy to the hut of the naked African, the Andean village, and the mainland and islands of Asia. His wife, Mary, was a happy creature who shared her husband's ideals.

I assume that Ambassador Martin brought to the Dominican Republic the State Department's opinions on the outcome of Dominican events. In Santo Domingo, elections were due, and the probabilities were that the winner would be the UCN. The State Department knew that in December of the previous year, 1961, the UCN had been the dominant force in the Dominican Republic and that it had demonstrated its strength in a strike that had toppled Rodríguez Echavarría's junta. But in June of 1962, and even much later, the State Department did not know the true picture, because its officials had not gone out into the countryside or visited the urban slums and therefore were not accurately informed on the change that was being wrought in the nation.

During my first meeting with Martin, I sketched an isosceles triangle, a figure I was accustomed to employing as an illustration of a cross section of Dominican society. Along the base, which was the longest side of the triangle, I indicated the peasant class. Above, on a parallel line, I showed the urban workers and unemployed. Above that, on a parallel but shorter line, I showed the lower, middle, and upper-stratum urban groups. I told Ambassador Martin that the PRD deliberately worked along the longest line and I cited a few figures. "We are sure that by December 20, we shall be able to count on no fewer than 500,000 votes, which would mean victory in eighteen provinces. And I want to point out that we always make our estimates on a conservative basis. If our opponents continue making the same mistakes that they have been making so far, we will hit 600,000 votes," I told him. When the count came in, we had 628,000 votes, and we won twenty-two provinces of the total of twenty-seven; the Civic Union managed to capture only four. A third party took a single seat.

How was it possible to predict the election outcome?

Because politics, which in other periods of history had been an art guided by the strange gift of divination, had become an art based on facts. Previously it had been at a stage like that of medicine before the introduction of such factors as laboratory analysis, X rays, instruments for gauging blood pressure, and electrical devices for graphically recording the functioning of brain and heart. Modern sociology, mass psychology, and the accurate analysis of a people's history transformed political activity from a simple art into something far more significant, into a science that required art in its practitioner, but not art alone.

Of course, Ambassador Martin listened to me, but he did not believe me. In September, the State Department still thought that the Civic Union would win the elections, although by this juncture conditions had undergone some change, and the PRD was given a slim chance. About that time, a friend sought me out to tell me that the United States and Venezuelan Ambassadors were trying to arrange a joint meeting with Fiallo and myself. I asked what the topic would be, and was told that Presidents Kennedy and Betancourt were concerned that the Dominican democracy that should emerge from this year's elections be able to stand on its own feet from the beginning. To assure themselves that this would be the case, they wanted Fiallo and me to make a pledge of honor before their Ambassadors, i.e., to their governments. An Ambassador, after all, is the personal representative of his President.

The Venezuelan and U.S. governments thought that the Dominican presidency had become a contest solely between Fiallo and me. The meeting was intended to assure the winner that the loser would support the incoming regime as the loyal opposition, an opposition that would uphold democratic principles and refrain from plots or pressures that might endanger the regime that would emerge from the December 20 elections.

We had taken great care in the PRD to avoid mentioning not only presidential but all other candidates as well. Candidates for national offices—President and Vice President— were to be chosen during the national party convention without any previous commitments. Thus, we were under no circumstances interested in making political deals. The PRD was not only a political party but also a school of democracy. And we wanted to teach democracy along the purest possible lines. Our national convention was scheduled for October 19. I could not assume that I would be the presidential candidate of my party because I was not the candidate at this time, nor did I know if I ever would be.

Fiallo's situation was not the same. Although the UCN had not held its convention, party spokesmen already had been campaigning openly, with Fiallo as the presidential nominee. He was, to a certain extent, morally authorized by his fellow party members to act as a presidential candidate.

I explained this problem to my friend, and told him that furthermore I considered the meeting pointless. If the PRD lost the election, the conduct of the party and all its leaders would be only what would be expected from a serious political organization, an organization interested more in creating and sustaining a Dominican democracy than in coming to power. We would always, no matter what happened, offer loyal opposition to the established regime. But in the light of the UCN's make-up and what the events of the past few months had foreshadowed, Fiallo would not be able to keep such a pledge if he made it. Socially and psychologically, Fiallo allowed himself to be swayed by party leaders; instead of directing them, he was directed by them. He appeared to be the representative rather than the leader of a social group bent on attaining power at any cost. If it won the elections, the UCN would use its power to the utmost; if it lost, it would then conspire to take over the government.

In summary, then, any pledge I might make in the party's name would serve no purpose because without it, if we lost the election we would act as a loyal opposition. On the other hand, a pledge by Fiallo would serve no purpose because even with it, if the UCN lost it would not act as a loyal opposition. What use would there be in setting up a meeting of the two Ambassadors and Fiallo?

But for eight or ten days my friend refused to leave me in peace, and finally he used an argument that had to impress me: Rómulo Betancourt, an old personal and political friend and one of Trujillo's victims, wanted the meeting to be held, and I could not refuse to accommodate him. I accepted.

The conference was to take place in the Venezuelan Embassy. If I wished to be accompanied, it must be by only one person. The same stipulation was made for Fiallo. I took along my PRD Secretary General, Angel Miolán, and as the appointment had been set for eight-thirty in the evening, we presented ourselves at the Embassy at eight-twenty-seven. After nine, a UCN leader arrived with the message that Fiallo was engaged and would be a little late. Actually, Fiallo arrived at about ten o'clock, with two people in tow.

Neither the PRD Secretary General nor the two UCN leaders were allowed to attend the meeting. Only Fiallo and myself, Ambassadors Izaguirre and Martin, and Martin's interpreter were permitted to participate.

The conference appeared to be very important to those who had arranged it. From the way Ambassador Martin spoke, I realized that the State Department attached extraordinary significance to the gathering. For a moment I thought that the idea had come not from President Betancourt but from the State Department, which had probably asked Betancourt to participate through his Ambassador in order to remove any shadow of what might be interpreted as American intervention in Dominican internal affairs. It was October. The PRD was growing all over the country. And already threats were being circulated that if the PRD won the elections, it would never govern. Had these threats reached Washington's ears?

In solemn language, which Mr. Fandino, his interpreter, translated meticulously. Ambassador Martin said that he was facing the future President of the Dominican Republic, since one of us, Fiallo or myself, was going to be elected on December 20. He spoke to us in the name of President Kennedy, to ask us to promise right here and now, tonight, that whoever lost the elections would bind himself to form a loyal opposition party. In the event that we agreed, he had with him a draft of the provisions of the pledge, and we had the authority to make changes. He had written the draft only to save time.

I explained that I was by no means there as the probable future President of the Republic, because the PRD had not yet nominated its presidential candidate. Therefore, I had no legal authority to make commitments as a candidate. I could, however, do so as President of my party, if everyone present was willing, but on one condition—that this meeting remained confidential. If the leaders of the other parties were to learn that two governments in the Americas believed so early in the game that the December elections were going to be decided between the PRD and the UCN, they would be up in arms and would accuse both the United States and Venezuela of interfering in internal affairs in order to favor two parties to the detriment of the rest. Both conditions were accepted.

Martin's draft contained five points, if I remember correctly. Izaguirre said that he knew them and had approved them. He asked if I had any objections, and I assured him that I had none but that I wanted the following to be understood: that the PRD accepted all five points as a gesture of courtesy and friendship toward the governments represented here by the two Ambassadors, because with or without these points the PRD, if it lost the elections, would follow the only political policy that could be expected from a serious party, that of a loyal opposition, with no underhanded attacks on the government. What we had done previously under the governments of Balaguer and the Council of State we would continue to do now—avoid any conspiracies or alignments with military factions so as not to open any political doors to them. The PRD understood, I said, that soldiers belonged in their barracks, and there they should remain.

Fiallo discussed a few of the points. There were, he said, details in the five points that he would like to improve on. He spoke as a President-elect would, although at one point he did me the favor of stating: "If Bosch wins, I am sure that I will not be forced into exile." (The UCN came to power by means of a *coup d'état* in September, 1963, and Fiallo's signature was the first to appear on the document defining the coup's government, and I am writing these pages in exile.)

At about the time of this meeting, General Rodríguez Reyes came to see me one night. He was Inspector of the Armed Forces and the only general then accorded a leader's status. He had entered the service as an ordinary soldier. He was to die that year, at the end of December, in the bloody Palmasola episode, quelling a peasant uprising. The General told me that strong internal pressures and tensions were operating in the Council of State, and its members were splitting into factions. One faction hoped to extend the Council's life by a year, and one member had proposed a *coup d'état* to him. He said that he had told the Councilor Yes, but he had immediately informed the high command of what had happened. He said that the Armed Forces would not allow themselves to be used for such tactics. A few days later, three high officials came to see me for the express purpose of confirming what Rodríguez Reyes had told me. I listened to them attentively, but without encouraging their recital. I did not wish to let them feel that they were actors in the political drama.

In actuality, although the PRD used these reports to keep the people vigilant, we attached no real importance to them. We knew that there would be no other route than the electoral one. The country was moving toward this, and with the passing of each day, increasing external pressure was exerted for holding the elections. It is a fact that the government was being manipulated from outside the country. The reins were in the hands of the OAS, which hoped that here would be an example for the rest of Latin America of a member republic that chose to solve its problems with democratic elections instead of resorting to violence.

The PRD national convention, starting October 19, was planned as a historic event. Never before in the history of the country had 500 men and women—all of them elected directly by fellow party members in all the towns and municipal districts—been brought together for the sole purpose of acting as true representatives of the voters. These people were going to frame a government program for the party, to nominate candidates for President and Vice President of the Republic, and to revise party statutes. Included in this group were lawyers, businessmen, doctors, dentists, engineers, farmers, peasants, laborers, teachers, housewives, domestic servants, and students, of all ages and races.

The Dominican Republic was about to celebrate the 120th anniversary of its founding, and it was the first time in all these years that Dominican delegates had convened in a democratic convention with no previous commitments of any kind, either open or concealed. It was the first time that men and women of the people had been gathered together to represent their communities. It was the first time that such representatives were going to discuss and formulate a government program. I know whereof I speak when I say that no convention in any democracy in the Americas

—even the United States—had ever been so pure in its objectives, or so truly representative. And I might add that this was the first time in their history that the Dominican people had had in their own hands the opportunity to exercise authority in the area of citizens' rights. I might add further that the fact that this was happening for the first time in the 120 years of the Republic provides the explanation for the 1963 *coup d'état*.

No matter how well a thing is carried out on the first attempt, a nation cannot assert its rights in a single display of will. Democratic freedom, like life itself, must be defended and improved day by day. And only after much time has gone by, when no member of the national community questions in his conscience whether or not that freedom is in danger—that is, when it has become as automatic and accepted as breathing—and when it is assured that the people's freedom is based on firm foundations, is this freedom inalienable, never again to be lost.

The world is at a critical stage. Perhaps in a few years the earnest desire of the PRD leaders to provide a lesson in democracy for the Dominican Republic will seem ridiculous. Perhaps even before I might think it possible, Dominicans of the next generation will laugh at that anachronistic goal, attempted at such an unpropitious hour, precisely when all the signs of the times heralded the last days of democracy. But we had dedicated an entire lifetime to an ideal. It was logical, then, that we should fulfill our political destiny with total fidelity. Man's duty as an individual and as a social being is to translate his convictions into reality, and he should discharge this duty even though he knows, as José Martí, the great Cuban liberator, once said, that he will never sit in the shade of the tree he has planted.

The national convention nominated me as the PRD's presidential candidate, by a vote of 499 to 1. The nomina-

tion of Buenaventura Sánchez as the vice-presidential candidate was faulty from the beginning, because it did not
fulfill the requisites of the Electoral Law. When we found
out that the UCN was waiting for the last minute—when
there would be no time in which to undo the damage
legally—to fight both candidacies on the basis of the de-
fects in the vice-presidential nomination, a second convention was held. It nominated Dr. Segundo Armando Gon-
zález Tamayo as the candidate for the vice presidency. A
young doctor from the lower-middle class, born in the
fields of Puerto Plata, a place no one had ever heard of
until it had become one of the first PRD chapters. It had
never previously been thought possible for a Dominican of
humble origins and without an illustrious name to be
nominated for one of the two highest offices in the land.
Unquestionably, the PRD had turned all the old notions
upside down, something that the UCN *tutumpotes* were
not disposed to forgive.

Immediately after the national convention, I withdrew
to a place where no member of the party could find me. I
wanted the conventions in the provinces and small towns
that were responsible for naming their provincial and municipal candidates to do so by themselves, on their own,
without having even the opportunity of consulting me. We
ran the risk that they might not always nominate the best
men available, but as one learns to walk by taking steps, so
democracy is learned by practicing it. If the provincial and
municipal assemblies chose badly now, they would choose
better the next time. "No one learns out of another's
head," the peasants say. This is a good rule to keep in mind.

One stage in the party's life ended with the conventions
that named candidates for senators, congressmen, and may-
ors, and another began. For years and years we had prepared ourselves in exile for the task that we had finished
that October. Miolán had been groomed for all the work

involved in mobilizing the masses. He had learned in Mexico and had observed in Cuba and in Venezuela how democratic processes function. He had learned to organize meetings, conventions, rallies; to draw up agendas, statutes, orders of the day; to direct the work of the leaders and the development of plans. For a year and four months, in which the days blurred into nights, he had carried the burden of the party's organization. In the next stage, which would last less than two months, he had to teach an entire nation the complicated mechanism of democratic elections, and he had to teach several thousand PRD members how to protect the people against all kinds of tricks that could ensnare them. The majority of these thousands of party members in need of training were from the masses. Only a few came from the lower stratum of the middle class, and fewer still from the middle stratum.

It was a vast job. But Angel Miolán did it. The credit goes to him, and also to his helpers, and to the people themselves, whose quickness in learning proved that they were ripe for growth. I say this on the record for the benefit of those who regard the common people of the Dominican Republic—the masses, the poor from the slums and the fields—as a group without the ability to improve their own fate.

Coup First and Elections Later

As November approached and the vigor of the PRD's growth became evident, the UCN began to trot out its carefully prepared tricks, using as its vehicle the organ of government, the Council of State. The Central Electoral Board announced that there would be no colored ballots. (When PRD lawyers subsequently revised the Electoral Law, they found the most curious article ever contained in any law: a paragraph to the effect that the ballots would be colored, with one color for each party, but that the Central Electoral Board was empowered to decree that all ballots be the same color. For the same article to direct one thing and then authorize the contrary must constitute an authentic case for "Believe It or Not" in the annals of the world's legislation.)

For the Dominican Revolutionary Party, the colored ballot was a matter about which there could be no two ways. The Dominican public is at least 50 per cent illiterate. Even people more or less educated who have not been faced with the ballot system for years will find it confusing to vote correctly. So imagine, if you will, the plight of the totally illiterate. The UCN, fully aware of these circumstances, launched a campaign to keep those unable to read or write from voting. Articles by a historian demanding such measures appeared in the UCN newspaper. I have in my files proof that those articles were published with Fiallo's full approval. If the PRD were to permit our first free elections, supervised by the OAS, to be held without colored ballots, it would set a precedent that the Dominican masses could never hope to see changed. The colored ballot was indispensable if the common people were to know for whom they were voting.

By this time, we had learned something that we had not realized soon enough—that the UCN dominance of the Central Electoral Board was so solid that if the PRD entered into a battle with the Board, it would lose. The PRD had already lost the fight for elections on behalf of constitutional revision because a Board member had alleged that a Revisory Constituent Assembly as a sovereign assembly would have the power to depose the Council of State. The mobilization of public opinion that we had effected was not enough. The Council of State had proved that the opinion of the masses did not matter, and so the PRD had to use other measures: We threatened to withdraw from the elections if colored ballots were not used.

The situation grew to crisis proportions. The military high command went before the Council of State with an ultimatum: "If there are no elections, the Armed Forces will take over as of February 27, 1963, and as stated in the Constitution, the Council of State is obliged to relinquish power on that date. That is, not one day later, but *on* February 27." The Council of State gave in. The President of the Central Electoral Board was called to the National Palace, and the following day a notice was posted announcing that there would be colored ballots, that three parties would have white ballots bordered with other colors and the fourth party would have an all-white ballot. Since the all-white ballot was to be the PRD's, if there was any confusion among the voters, we would come out on the short end. We accepted the decision, even though it was to our disadvantage, because the PRD felt that the most important consideration was the continuance of a custom that had been practiced up to this time. In the long run, forty or fifty thousand votes meant little to us. According to our calculations, we would have at least 200,000 votes more than the runner-up.

But why had the military, which only a few months later was to abolish the Constitution, acted as it had?

At that time, the generals and colonels were very much on the defensive. Many of them had been publicly accused of committing crimes in Trujillo's regime. They feared a political crisis that would throw them out of their barracks and place them within reach of the public. In the rank and file of the Armed Forces and the police, there were constantly small and even big rebellions. A few months before, the police had refused to accept as their chief an officer appointed by the Council of State. (Ten months later, in September, 1963, those same military chiefs were in a different position. They found themselves under the control of a government that permitted them no privileges, that prohibited them from continuing to collect 10- or 15-percent commissions on goods purchased by the military, that did not appoint the relatives recommended for public offices, that no longer provided them with automobiles, clothing, and furniture.) In November of 1962, the military leaders wanted security, and to get it, they assumed the role of defenders of the Constitution. (In September of 1963, they wanted privileges that a constitutional government was not prepared to grant them. In this instance, the Constitution was an obstruction.) Moreover, if the PRD withdrew from the 1962 elections, the victory would go to the UCN. And the military high command feared having the UCN in power because they had been Ramfis Trujillo's accomplices and supporters, and the UCN had been a decisive force in the fight against Ramfis. (By 1963 the UCN was siding with the military and was linked to the plans for the coup.)

The military chiefs changed their position and opinions between November, 1962, and September, 1963. This happens often enough in countries like the Dominican Republic, in which the social organization is so primitive and the social structure is so weak.

The UCN *tutumpotes* had lost the battle of legal tricks. Now they changed their tactics and poured all their efforts into a campaign for a *coup d'état,* which they finally brought off in September, 1963. Although they certainly did not formulate it in these words, their political slogan was "Coup First and Elections Later." The groundwork was laid by the coup's leitmotiv, which began appearing in November: "The PRD Is Communist."

The technique employed was the following: A newspaper in Puerto Rico published a "report" that Thelma Frías, a PRD leader and senatorial candidate from the National District, had removed a painting of the Virgin of Altagracia from the place where the PRD's national convention had been held. The "report" had been concocted in the UCN's offices. Fiallo immediately used this "report from foreign newspapers" in a radio talk. Trujillo had used the same technique, publishing abroad what he was later going to use for propaganda within the country. Monsignor Pérez Sánchez, a member of the Council of State and of the Church's hierarchy, declared that Thelma Frías' act was equivalent to replacing the coat-of-arms on the country's flag with a hammer and sickle. And following the propaganda tactic that Trujillo had made classic, the UCN radio asserted again and again that Thelma Frías had asked that instead of the coat-of-arms, the Communist hammer and sickle be placed on the flag.

If the PRD counted among its leaders one dedicated enemy of Communism, it was Thelma Frías. She took part daily in the party radio program called *Democratic Tribune* and on one occasion in July, when she had devoted her time almost exclusively to dealing with the situation in Cuba, she had been so vehement that I had had to have a personal talk with her. "Remember," I scolded, "that for the Dominican people, such ardent anti-Communism is almost synonymous with Trujillo, who conducted such a frenzied anti-Communist campaign. If the PRD imitates Trujillo in this, people will become frightened of us. You must keep in mind," I went on, "that for the Dominican people, the bitterest memory is that left by Trujilloism." She accepted my advice, but not docilely because she forcefully defended her position. Nevertheless, she was singled out as a scapegoat for the launching of the campaign that would lay the groundwork for the *coup d'état*. This was explainable because in the neighborhoods of the capital, Thelma Frías was remarkably popular.

Suddenly, around the end of November and the beginning of December, the voices from the pulpits poured over the land. Many priests began preaching, in the cities and the countryside, that the PRD was either Communist, Communist-influenced, or Communist-led. One fine day, a concrete accusation materialized: that I was a Communist, a Marxist-Leninist, and furthermore that this was vouched for by a Jesuit priest, Rev. Láutico García. Santa María Radio, which belongs to the Catholic Church and is located in Santo Cerro de La Vega—a sort of Mecca for Dominican Catholics—announced that if I won the elections, all the nation's priests would die on their altars, that Dominican children would be snatched up and packed off to Russia, from whence they would return converted into enemies of God. The slogan "Coup First and Elections Later" was on the march. The upper-middle class and the first families flagrantly declared that even if the PRD won the elections, it could not govern because they would never permit it to take over.

I realized then that Trujillo's ghost had returned from the beyond to resume command of the country. On the pretext that he had to destroy Communism, Trujillo had killed, raped, burned, tortured, and plundered. Now, on that same pretext, he had returned to the land that he had martyred and convoked his followers to revive the past. In a short story I had written many years before, probably around 1943 or 1944, called "The Dead Still Live" ("El difunto estaba vivo"), I had tried to carry out the theme that the past is difficult to extinguish because the past lives on in the present if there is a single man still living who reacts to the sentiments or ideals that preceded him. In December of 1962, the UCN and the priesthood had, figuratively speaking, opened the dictator's tomb and he had come out and returned to take possession of the country. The people, however, could not see it; the people do not see something that does not have a body. For them, Trujillo was buried in Paris, and Ramfis and his uncles were in exile.

From April 5, 1958, until April 4, 1961, I had been living in Venezuela. Around mid-1959, if I remember correctly, at the request of Julio César Martínez, another Dominican exile, who had taken over the editorship of a magazine called *Momento,* I had written three articles dealing purely with political science. These articles had provoked letters from readers and even a biting response from a Communist journalist who had accused me of holding back the future Dominican revolution. Rómulo Betancourt, then President of Venezuela, had asked me to augment the short series, as in his opinion my articles were too few to cover the political theme as fully as it deserved. After an exile of some years, Martínez came back to Santo Domingo and resumed publication of his weekly, *Renovación,* which had been closed down in the Trujillo days. He reprinted several of those articles, and it was on one of these that Father Láutico García based his accusation that I was Marxist-Leninist.

Political science is the study of the systems and philosophies of government that mankind has produced. Another form of political activity involves saying this or that about a government or accusing a leader of this or that. Political science had been debated in Venezuela since the days of Bolívar's wars. Bolívar himself often expressed political concepts that were truly original, and he could do this because he had an audience more or less equipped to understand him. This was not the case in the Dominican Republic, where, with the exception of the nineteenth century thinker Eugenio María de Hostos, no one ever spoke the language of political science, but rather one spoke the idiom of politics, which meant either slandering or defending with ardent fanaticism. At best, someone might mention measures necessary to improve the country's lot, but no one, as far as I know, had ever touched on the political concepts that man had created over the long span of human history. In a modest way, within the limits of my knowledge, I had done this in Venezuela. But what I had done in Venezuela with the approval and encouragement of the people, leaders, and democratic intellectuals, was treated in Santo Domingo as evidence that I was a Communist. Beyond any doubt, the shadow of Trujillo had returned to take control of the land.

From my position, the situation looked bad. Elections were only a few days away. The two Communist parties, the PSP and the MPD, had urged abstention from the elections, and the 14th of June had let itself be swayed by their argument. If the PRD abstained from the elections, it would confirm what many people suspected, that we were Communists. But if we went ahead with the elections and lost, we would never, ever shake off the Marxist-Leninist label.

The great masses of the Dominican public could certainly be influenced by this propaganda. To a worker or to one of the thousands of unemployed who occasionally earned a peso in some chance job, anti-Communism was not what it was to the people of upper, middle, or lower stratum of the middle class. In Trujillo's days, when a laborer asked for a 10-centavo increase in his daily wage, he was killed as a Communist. When a poor farmer sought to defend his property from Trujillo's confiscation, he was hanged as a Communist. The men and women of the people feared anti-Communism as one aspect of Trujilloism, and the one most used to justify the greatest cruelties. But there was one important difference between Communism and anti-Communism. To the people, Trujillo's militant anti-Communism was distasteful. However, the idea that I might be a Communist could frighten them just as much as it would have frightened them if I had been a professional Communist-hunter.

The priesthood had perhaps a decisive influence over the upper stratum of the middle class, and considerable sway over the middle and lower strata. But its influence was practically absolute over certain farm areas—which could account for 100,000 votes. The Church was equally strong among the Armed Forces high command, where its authority could be invoked to encourage soldiers to spread the false tale of our Communist leanings throughout the countryside from which they sprang. But the Church did not influence the masses of workers and the unemployed, and these constituted the PRD's most solid voting bloc.

Our campaign against the 14th of June had been relatively simple because Catorcitas recruited most of their militants from youth of the middle and upper strata of the middle class. Such was not the case with the PRD. In any event, propaganda by the priesthood could not weaken the PRD to the point of reducing it to a second-rank party. Nevertheless, if the Church swayed the rural vote, we could very well lose the elections by a narrow margin.

If the propaganda from the pulpits and the confessionals had been simply anti-PRD, the harm it was doing us would have been tolerable. But it went beyond these limits, far beyond, and accused us of being Communists. For example, in La Vega, a city situated in the heart of a strongly Catholic area, a priest refused to give a Mass requested by a group of PRD youngsters on the ground that "the PRD is Communist."

The priests had loosed against the PRD the sacred tongue of the Psalms, a tongue that should have been reserved solely for glorifying Our Lord and propagating religion. However, the priests had not said that Dominicans should vote for the UCN or the Social Christians. They simply said that I, the PRD's candidate, was a Communist. To counter such an accusation authorized by God's representatives in this world of miseries, I would have to show the public that the priests were not telling the truth. It was not an easy task.

The PRD National Executive Committee asked the Catholic leadership to clarify the situation. Church authorities answered with a communiqué that clarified nothing, and that confused everyone all the more. The Dominican Church hierarchy simply washed its hands of the matter, as Pontius Pilate had done while the Pharisees had screamed for Barrabas.

We quickly devised an emergency strategy. I would withdraw as presidential candidate. If, in spite of this, the

Church refused to disavow Father García, I would invite him to join me in a television debate. Because of the possibility that he might receive orders not to accept the challenge to a discussion, I would proffer my invitation at the last minute, when the Catholic authorities would be conscious of the responsibilty they would have to bear in case the PRD should not be in the elections.

Salvador Pittaluga, the sponsor of a television program, realized that this was the opportunity of a lifetime for him, one that might never come his way again, and he spoke personally with Father García. Pittaluga's idea was to select as moderator an intellectual of prestige, but I suggested that he himself fill this role. The priest accepted through Pittaluga, but imposed one condition: that the discussion should touch only on the subject at hand—whether or not I was a Marxist-Leninist. I accepted, of course.

The TV debate lasted several hours, with the whole country hanging on its progress. It was broadcast simultaneously on radio, and probably more than a million Dominicans were glued to radio or TV sets until about two o'clock in the morning. Many women made vows to go to Santo Cerro, the Holy Mount, and to Higuey—the two principal Dominican shrines—to take the habit, pay for Masses and candles, and do penance if Father García did not come out the winner that night. So it is that for many of the faithful, the religion preached by the priests serves to soothe the anguish that the priests cause them.

Father García was a Spaniard. Knowing this, I brought to the television studio the dictionary of the Royal Academy of Spain, certain that he would not contradict it. With that dictionary, it could be determined if the Father was telling the truth in accusing me of being a Marxist-Leninist. From his interpretation of the articles on which he had based his accusation, one thing was clear: The priest had taken the words in their everyday sense. Not realizing that those articles dealt with pure political science, he had not taken the words in their strict scientific sense.

Before that broadcast, a large number of people of the middle and lower strata of the middle class had refused to tune in on my radio chats. They felt that I was a demagogue. They listened to the UCN and the other parties claim that I spoke for the mob, for the plebeians only, in the vernacular of the lowest classes. But that night they listened to me because they hoped to hear García crush me with his cleverness, the traditional cleverness of the Jesuits. And that same night, although it was not my original intention, the circumstances demanded that I speak in the language taught me by the distinguished authors of the treatises on political and social science, which I had read for years. And so it happened that night that several thousand Dominicans finally discovered who the PRD candidate really was. When the debate was over, there were at least 50,000 more PRD supporters than on the day that Monsignor Pérez Sánchez initiated the offensive by the priesthood, based on the ingenious accusation that Thelma Frías had been guilty of something tantamount to replacing the coat-of-arms in the flag with the hammer and sickle.

Father García had tenaciously refused to concede that I was not a Communist, but I felt that here, in the television studio, the entire nation was accusing him of refusing to admit something that was evident in their eyes. Father García had no more arguments to support his position, but still he did not give in. Soon he began quoting passages from a book. When he had finished, I said, "I never wrote that in my life, Father."

"No," he admitted. "You never wrote this—but Angel Miolán did."

García himself had demanded, through Pittaluga, that the debate be strictly limited to the accusation against me, and only me, and I had accepted. But now the priest, perhaps without realizing it, was furthering the strategy of "Coup First and Elections Later." It was so late in the game—this was the night of December 18, and the elections were set for the twentieth—that it was impossible to prevent the elections and the PRD victory. But there was still time to lay the foundation for the future coup. The rumor that "Juan Bosch is not a Communist but Angel Miolán is" was to play an important role in that coup.

The fact is, Miolán had never been a Communist. He had belonged to APRA, the American Revolutionary Popular Alliance (Alianza Popular Revolucionaria Americana), in fact. Anyone versed in the ins and outs of political affiliations in Latin America knows that APRA and Communism occupy positions as opposed as the Evangelists and Catholics were years ago. The two latter groups are derived from a belief in Christ, to be sure, as the Apristas and the Communists both originated from the philosophy of Karl Marx. The socio-political language in almost all the modern political parties of the Western world is so similar that the Socialists in Europe, the Apristas in Peru, the Revolutionaries in Mexico, the Democratic Action Party in Venezuela, and the Liberals in Colombia all speak of the proletariat, the class struggle, the bourgeoisie, imperialism, and social revolution. In those pages, written by Miolán in Mexico in 1938 or 1939, when all Mexico was shaken by the revolutionary impetus, there was not the slightest hint of Communism.

Father García finally admitted that I was not a Communist, but he left in the air, like a venomous vapor, the idea that Miolán was. In short, the plan to overthrow our government was already a seed in the ground that would not take long to sprout. "Coup First and Elections Later." And that is just how it all came out, although in the eyes of the people it seemed that the elections came first and the coup later.

The Role of the Church
in the Coup

Father Láutico García had admitted that I was not a Communist, but the priests who constituted the vanguard of the anti-PRD offensive refused to give way. On the contrary, they were to organize their battle plan as soon as the elections were over, and keep up the fight even after the constitutional government had been toppled. Since I realized that it would be like that, I did not consider Father García's admission that I was not a Communist a sign of peace. "Do you persist in refusing the presidential candidacy?" asked moderator Pittaluga in the final moment of the television interview. I answered: "I do not wish to be a candidate because I know the PRD will win the elections, and if it does, the government I head will not be able to rule. It will be overthrown in a short time on the pretext that it is Communist."

Yet by this time it was impossible to renounce my candidacy. Outside the television studio, a cheering crowd was waiting. In the slum neighborhoods, all the streets were as alive as if it were daytime, although it was two in the morning. In every corner of the country, hundreds of thousands of enthusiastic PRD members were waiting to cast their vote a scant thirty hours later. I had to bow to this mass pressure. If I regret anything in my life, it is my agreeing to go into that election as the party's presidential candidate while knowing beyond the slightest shadow of a doubt that the government I was to head would be toppled, perhaps even before it came to power.

"The world is divided into two groups—those who love and construct, and those who hate and destroy," José Martí had said. The hatred of the first-family caste toward the common people, a hatred operating through the medium of a middle class without purpose, without principles, without patriotism, without love, was going to destroy in a short time all that the people had built up out of their democratic faith. All that the people of the elite had learned at the University of Santo Domingo and foreign universities, the books they had read, the degrees they had received, was turned to this destructive task. A leader of a political *ventorrillo* tossed out this strange theory: "These elections are not valid because Juan Bosch deceived the public."

The day on which I was to assume the presidency was still some distance off, and yet the democratic doctrine was being horribly and incredibly twisted. It is accepted that political doctrines are the product of social pacts arrived at by an express or tacit agreement of the society. Furthermore, it is accepted that all these doctrines, without exception, acknowledge that each has an agreed-on starting point, however dogmatic its results—and its innate character—and that there is no way known to man of founding a political system without this fundamental agreement. The democratic system starts from one point: that sovereignty resides with the people alone and that what they decide by majority wish is sacred. This *should* be unreservedly admitted everywhere. In short, a representative democracy cannot exist unless it is accepted that the will of the people, expressed freely, legitimately, and honestly, is the very essence of the system.

The Dominican elections of December 20, 1962, supervised by the OAS, were never criticized at the time, wholly or in part, by any of the various participating political groups. Throughout the American continent, they were jubilantly acclaimed as model elections. Nevertheless, a presidential candidate who had received a bare 1 per cent of the vote charged that "The elections are not valid because Juan Bosch deceived the public." His meaning was that the people had voted for the PRD because I had tricked them into it. The author of this innovation in the doctrine of democratic representative government had been exiled by the Trujillo regime for more than twenty-five years, was a graduate of the Sorbonne medical school, had been a professor of philosophy at a Venezuelan university, and was the author of several books. This illustrious reformer of a doctrine with almost 200 years of application behind it in the most advanced countries of the West had discovered, to the glory of the Dominican intelligentsia, that anybody who wins an election has deceived the public. If this be true, what label would be attached to someone who wins with more than 60 per cent of the total vote? Such was the case of the PRD. This could only make us criminals of the lowest order, far worse than those who win by a narrower margin, since we had deceived a larger proportion of the voters. This extraordinary discovery was made, as chance would have it, by a Dominican from the first families, the grandson and great-grandson of Dominican Presidents.

Now then, why had a handful of foreign priests, neither

Dominican nor elite, so enthusiastically shouldered the task of preventing the development of Dominican democracy? Who was behind all this? What unseen power on these or any other shores gave the orders? What masters were these men serving?

Perhaps they were serving many masters at the same time. Spanish and Dominican Jesuits, as well as young Dominicans of other congregations, had their own political position. They were Social Christians, and they wanted, if not a victory for that group, at least a showing at the polls good enough to place a few of their men in congressional and municipal posts. In broad terms, the Social Christian priests were in no way plotting a *coup d'état*. But neither is it fair to say that they were backing the constitutional government.

Another faction, made up of the older Dominican clergy and foreigners who were long-time residents of the country, including higher-ups in the Dominican Church, acted like members of the first families or of the upper-middle class. (One of them, an American, wrote to *The New York Times* after the *coup d'état* and repeated, on a higher level, what Monsignor Pérez Sánchez had asserted ten months earlier.) UCN agents in Miami spread reports that the Dominican Government was organizing a secret militia of 40,000 men, although no one with an ounce of sense would believe that such a secret militia could be organized in a climate of complete freedom of press, radio, and movement. Fiallo said in an article, possibly an open letter, that I was organizing such a militia in order to destroy the Armed Forces. And Monsignor Thomas Reilly, the Bishop of San Juan de la Maguana, confirmed this in *The New York Times* with genuinely priestly truthfulness.

Another group of the Dominican clergy, the smallest but most active, wholeheartedly dedicated itself to conspiracy. What is more, the Rasputin of the *coup d'état* of September 25 was a Creole priest who had devoted most of his life of the cloth to performing public services on Trujillo's orders.

In the elections of December 20, 1962, Congressmen and their alternates had been elected. According to the law that governed the elections, the Congressmen would make up the Revisory Constituent Assembly, and if that body did not complete its task by February 27, 1963—the date on which the officials elected on December 20 were to take their seats—their alternates would serve in the Chamber of Deputies until the Congressmen finished revising the Constitution. I was traveling in Europe at the time, but if I remember correctly, the Revisory Assembly met by the middle of January. The newspaper *El Caribe* published a kind of draft of the PRD's projected Constitution, and as it did not mention the Concordat that Trujillo had made with the Holy See, it aroused the wrath of Avernus, precipitating a spectacle worthy of a place in Dominican history. Children from Catholic schools stoned the Congress building and broke windows. Thus did history repeat, for something similar had happened in the early days of Christianity, when the preachers of the Word were stoned by multitudes made up mostly of children. Children, as everyone knows, are so rational, so in command of their actions, so organized! They never do what their elders, parents, or teachers tell them to do; they only do what they themselves believe is holy and good for humanity.

Trujillo's last Constitution—there were many Constitutions during his regime—was a treasure house of constitutional oddities. One of its articles declared untouchable, beyond seizure and beyond human, judicial, or other reach any properties held by any President of the Republic or his widow or heirs. That same Constitution provided that relations between the Catholic Church and the Dominican State were to be governed by the Concordat that Trujillo had signed with the Pope. This meant that the governments that succeeded Trujillo's were powerless to act in vital areas of Dominican life—among them public education, vital for the country's future. Constitutional rights, then, were fossilized, and their evolution was out of the question. On the other hand, if the Dominican Constitution provided that relations between Church and State were to be subject to the Concordat, why not similarly include in the Constitution the many other international treaties that the Republic was committed to?

The last Trujillo Constitution had been amended under Balaguer's regime in order to create the Council of State, and again under the government of the Council of State in order to call for the 1962 elections. Thus the Council of State was obligated to hold elections because of its own amendment. But in neither Balaguer's nor the Council of State's amendments had the Concordat been touched on. And the Holy See was not disposed to yield in this matter. Before I ascended to the presidency, the Papal Nuncio, Monsignor Emanuele Clarizio, came to see me to demand that I ask the Revisory Assembly to retain the article referring to the Concordat. "Monsignor, you know what a democracy is," I told him. "A democracy is not a regime governed by a single man, as was the case in Trujillo's era. I have no legal authority over the Constituent Deputies, but you know that they have been yielding in many matters. Go to see the President of the Assembly, Dr. Rafael Molina Ureña; talk with him, move your friends to action. Help us to create a Dominican democracy in which the institutions run on the fuel of public opinion." Some two months later, I used the same words to answer Monsignor Reilly, the Bishop of San Juan de la Maguana, who had also asked me to intervene in the matter of the constitutional revision, and who, being an American, ought to have understood how the democratic system works.

I could not explain either of these requests, Monsignor Clarizio's or Monsignor Reilly's, as being simply the result of custom. From 1930 until the present, everything accomplished in the Dominican Republic had been done by the will of the ruling power—first Trujillo's, then Balaguer's, finally the Council of State's. My thesis in "The Dead Still Live" was correct. But that thesis extended a great deal further than I had imagined when I wrote that story, as the two Monsignors were neither Dominican nor Spanish. If they had been Dominican, it could be explained that their outlook had been dictated by thirty-two years under a dictatorship. If they had been Spanish, it could be explained that they were acting like Dominicans. What, then, was happening? Apparently without being aware of it, they were obeying a powerful impulse that although not very clearly defined had placed many priests in opposition to the masses in the PRD's following. Probably without realizing it, they were behaving like members of the Dominican upper-middle class. The Catholic hierarchy in the country lived in the same atmosphere as the elite and the upper-middle class, and had no contact with or knowledge of the masses. It had no notion that they constituted a social class that aspired to something beyond what it then represented. The clergy knew this social group only as poor people, who were given alms from time to time and who should be conquered in the name of the faith. The lofty Catholic hierarchy was no greater than the milieu in which it lived.

When the new Constitution was promulgated, on April 29, 1963, the Church declined to send a representative to the official ceremony. This was a gesture of rebellion condemned by the Church itself, since the Church maintains as doctrine respect for legally established institutions and governments. But the high Church officials in the Dominican Republic acted like those on the level of society in which they moved. There, the people of the elite and the upper stratum of the middle class said that this Constitution was invalid because it had been drafted by "unimportant" and "ignorant" people. Just imagine! The Revisory Assembly included laborers, students, housewives— people whose names had never been heard in the chic drawing rooms of the nation's socialites. Truly this was unpardonable in a representative democracy with more than 3 million people, of whom scarcely 2 million were farmers and perhaps only another 700,000 or 800,000 were laborers and the unemployed. It was not right to pay attention to these few. The Revisory Constituent Assembly, the Congress, and the judiciary and executive positions should all be filled with men from among the 100 illustrious families. They were, in truth, the only citizens with the right to represent the people. The people should never have voted for the PRD, and since they had done what they should not have done, they must be punished and held up as an example to future generations.

The 1963 Constitution was nothing out of this world, but it had some daring aspects: it dared to omit mention of the Concordat; to establish that workers had the right to participate in the profits of the companies employing them; to state that the law would set the maximum limits on individual holdings of agricultural lands; to declare that a citizen's rights were inviolable.

A constitutional provision intended to assure democracy within the unions specified that in all shops and factories, only a single union would be permitted—whichever one represented the majority of members. This caused a great furor. It was held to be tantamount to constitutional authorization of a single centralized union—in other words, Communism. While I was President, objections from the United Nations Human Rights Commission reached me one after another, denouncing such dictatorial action by the Dominican Government. But the government had had nothing to do with writing the Constitution; its only role was to respect it and make it respected. Moreover, the authors of this controversial provision had had no intention of establishing a single centralized union. Each union was free to affiliate with whichever central body it felt would best further its interests. The wording of the article was merely intended to prevent the creation of company unions, by which the bosses could organize a union favorable to their interests and preclude the organization of a union that would genuinely respond to the needs of the majority of the workers.

The 1963 Dominican Constitution was timid, and conservative compared with, for example, the 1940 Cuban Constitution. But the ghost of Trujillo had been raised from the tomb months before and had taken command of the upper stratum of the middle class. Trujillo, now as a ghost, was again "the Chief" as in the years before May 30, 1961. The ghost gave orders, and the old subordinates and partners and accomplices carried them out without a murmur. This Constitution would not be permitted to rule the nation, because despite its timidity and conservatism, it was an anti-Trujillo Constitution that made it possible for the many to dominate the few. It put an end to arbitrary imprisonment, deportation, torture, and plundering of property. It prevented any reintroduction of the gigantic landholdings that were familiar in the old days of the dictatorship, and the enslavement of the worker, who risked being killed as an accused Communist if he presumed to ask for a raise in wages. This Constitution guaranteed freedom from paid informers, freedom of speech, freedom of assembly, freedom of movement—which had been very dangerous activities for many who daily carried out such activities in secret. It was the Constitution of a democracy, and democracy does not recognize privileges of the cradle or the bankbook—all of which is considered criminal in a country that earned social privileges by birth and economic privileges by a dictator's favor. Therefore, after the coup of September 25, 1963, along with the municipal governments, Congress, and the executive and judiciary powers, the 1963 Constitution was abolished by a stroke of the pen.

For the Catholic hierarchy, the 1963 Constitution had no validity; they refused to honor it in public. But while they did not accept it, neither did they publicly reject it. They simply pretended that it did not exist. However, many priests went a step further; they plotted to overthrow the constitutional government and, along with it, the institutions consecrated by that Constitution.

The day after the elections, the Air Force chaplain asked the officer at the San Isidro base to keep me under strict surveillance. He said that I was a Communist, and as soon as I put my hands on a member of the Armed Forces, I should be overthrown; otherwise, I would end up totally destroying the military. On July 16, I explained in one of the radio chats with which I kept the people informed about government activities, that I had asked that that priest be defrocked. "Bad chaplain, bad priest," I said. He was a bad chaplain because he had failed to limit his functions to religious matters and had invaded the area of politics. And he was a bad priest because he had disobeyed the Church he served, which ordered every Catholic to respect a legally constituted government. "Render therefore unto Caesar the things which are Caesar's, and unto God the things that are God's," Jesus had said. In Christ's time, Caesar had been the head of a state. Jesus had not come into the world to transform governments or to subvert states or to organize political coups, but rather to tell of the Kingdom of His Father, who was not of this world.

At the beginning of August, the Dominican Bishops— one Spanish and the other American—declared that each home in the land was in a state of distress, that the Republic could not continue in this fashion, that the Catholic bloc must save the people from the threat of Communism. From the first days of the constitutional government, foreign correspondents had been saying the same thing, and already Fiallo had loosed his black bull of fear into the arena. The government, according to Fiallo, was infiltrated with Communists at the highest level. Propaganda about the Communist menace had reached such an intensity that some Dominicans expected from one hour to the next that Fidel Castro's militiamen or Nikita Khrushchev's Cossacks would be upon them. Aggression would have had to originate outside the country because there were too few Communists within our borders to stand off even fifty policemen armed with blackjacks and tear-gas bombs.

After the Bishops' declaration, "Christian demonstrations" began, as if by magic. The first took place in the capital, and according to the newspaper *Listín Diario*, there were 40,000 demonstrators. The Chief of Police, from whom I had requested an accurate estimate, assured me that there had been fewer than 10,000. His figure must have been closer to the truth, because the site of the rally could not accommodate more than ten or twelve thousand people. The series of "Christian demonstrations" spread to other sections of the country, occurring at the rate of about one a week. As the number of demonstrations mounted, the size of the crowds dropped. At the last rally, fewer than 200 participated.

The use of Christ to agitate against the constitutional government was unfortunate for the Church, which thereby lost prestige. But this tactic served to justify the coup, and the coup enhanced Church power sufficiently to restore its lost prestige.

Months after the September coup, the priests maintained even in their confessionals that anyone who had not taken an active part in the coup was a Communist. One Spanish priest, a professor of Apologetics in a girls' school, commented during a discourse on hypocrisy: "An example of a hypocritical person is Juan Bosch, who tried to pass himself off as a democratic leader when all the time he was a Communist."

This is an admirable method of indoctrinating children with the notion that democracy and Communism are one and the same, that they seek the same ends, that they are two sides of the same coin, and that they should be despised and exterminated.

Might it not be possible that the Communists, in their infinite wisdom, disguised their cleverest agitators as priests?

Communism and Democracy

Of course, there were priests who were in no way involved in conspiracy and perhaps it would be fairer to say that many priests were not involved. I felt quite certain that even in the topmost reaches of the hierarchy, there were those who refused to be conspirators. But there were very few priests who were militant in defense of the government that the people had been given. These few were principally humble village priests, true representatives of the lower-middle class, who were closer to the masses than the majority of the Catholic clergymen.

In the Dominican Republic, as in Cuba, creole priests were in the minority, in contrast to the Spaniards, at least in recent years. And Spanish priests, with the exception of an occasional order such as the Franciscans, tended to live among the upper-middle class. They limited their activities to that sector, to establishing schools for children of *tutompotes* and to building chapels in elegant neighborhoods. As it happened, these priests had had virtually no political education. Even a Jesuit—and the Jesuits had been given political preparation—Father Láutico García, had called a Communist a man such as I, who had dedicated almost half his life to the fight for democracy, and not only in the Dominican Republic, but also in other countries of Latin America.

The priesthood was really influential with the masses only in a single area—a wholly farming region—north of La Vega, populated mostly by small landholders and farm laborers. Religion had a hold here because of an exceptional priest, the type that people identify with the noblest of the saints. His name was Father Fantino, and he was Italian. He had directed a semi-private school in La Vega, where he had educated at least a full generation. He was extremely well versed in Latin and grammar, and had a pioneer's spirit. He became increasingly drawn toward the spiritual rather than the educational, however, and finally left for Santo Cerro, the Holy Mount, taking his school with him. There, little by little, he won the genuine respect of the entire region for his sincere conduct in the service of God. I remember seeing him once at Mass, transfigured by religious passion, his hands folded over his chest, his eyes closed, the stamp of faith indelibly on his face. When he addressed the flock, his voice was truly celestial in tone. He had a large head and a big nose, and his whole head trembled. His garb was extremely humble, and at times there were stains on his habit. I was young then, but I often said: "After his death, Father Fantino will be worshiped throughout this region as a saint, and the people will have a piece of his cassock as a holy relic." And so it turned out.

Father Fantino is the reason for the influence of the Catholic Church throughout the region where he preached, by example. And he offers also an explanation for why the Catholic Church was elsewhere less influential than would be expected in a Catholic nation. On my campaign trips, I more than once saw a Spanish priest arriving at a country chapel. In each case the same scene was repeated: a few humble women at the door, sometimes having waited for a long time; the priest drives up in an automobile and gets out, carrying a small suitcase; he walks in without speaking to these women, without asking about their children and their husbands, or if there is anyone ill at home; he just strides into the little temple, often enough shouting: "*Vamos, vamos!*" A few minutes later he begins the Mass, chanting rapidly or not at all. If he has time, he hears a few confessions. Then he goes into the little sacristy to remove his vestments, and finally he hurries back into his car.

With such priests, the Church has little hope of exerting influence over the masses. On the other hand, with priests dedicated to cultivating the friendship of the middle class, especially the upper stratum, the Church will always be a political factor. Because politics is the staff of life for the upper stratum, its means of preserving or obtaining privileges. In the realm of religion, the Church has little influence on the Dominican people; in the realm of politics, there is much about the Church that the people dislike. Carried along by the feelings of the group in which it functions, the Church of the Dominican Republic can overthrow a democratic government. But what happens when it has to confront a great public galvanized by political passion? The answer was revealed by what happened after Father Láutico García charged that I was a Communist. The country reacted in a manner wholly opposite to that anticipated by the accusers.

In the upper stratum—with the usual exceptions, of course—a furor broke out at the mere idea of a Constitution which said that workers had a right to share in corporate profits. The editor of *El Caribe,* a newspaperman who had lived for many years in Puerto Rico, could not be—nor was he—either a fool or an ignoramus. Nevertheless, that man told me around mid-February of 1963, before I had been inaugurated as President, that he had already seen the *coletillas* in the articles and news items that his newspaper would print. A *coletilla* (literally, a small pigtail, a postscript) was a brief commentary by the printers' union that was inserted at the end of articles or news unfavorable to Fidel Castro printed in Cuban papers during the early months of the revolution. The same practice had been used in other Communist countries. And the *El Caribe* editor told me openly, in front of several people of the upper-middle class and even some industrialists, that the government I was about to head would be Communist. He *must have known* that Communists never ascend to power through elections, that Communists never draft constitutions except after liquidating all economic and political resistance, that Communists never set up congresses or give guarantees to unions or permit freedom for the opposition. He did not make his statement because he was ignorant or crazy. He knew how a democracy functions and could not pretend that, like many Dominicans, he had never lived under a democratic regime.

Nevertheless, I sometimes wonder if the editor of *El Caribe* and so many others of his social group did know what a democracy is. Often I find myself doubting whether the millions and millions of people born under a democratic system, and reared under it, really know what it means. In the days of the overthrow of the constitutional Dominican Government, *Life* magazine reported in its U.S. edition that my ministers had to consult me even in order to spend 300 pesos ($300). To me, this only indicated that the United States journalist writing for a magazine with a circulation of many millions was unaware that in a democratic regime a federal budget voted at the beginning of each fiscal year specifies, item by item, the amount that each government department can spend and on what it can spend it. Now, if a political commentator from the United States who writes for millions of readers, and who receives a substantial number of dollars in salary and expenses for writing about the Dominican Republic, is so uninformed about the financial operation of a democratic regime, perhaps it is possible that a Dominican journalist can know nothing of how the democratic system functions and therefore cannot know the doctrine of democracy. It is also possible, and for greater reason, that a Spanish priest might call a democratic leader a Communist.

But if I sometimes doubt the capacity of people to understand what democracy is, I more often tell myself that certain people behave in a truly irresponsible manner. Those charged with guiding the community, whether priests or journalists, cannot and should not ignore anything as important to human society as its political organization. A newspaperman from a democratic country, or from a country aspiring to become democratic, and a Catholic priest from any country are obliged to know thoroughly and in detail not only what democracy is and how it functions, but also what Communism is and how it functions. The journalist, the author of books, the professor, the priest who does not know what democracy is and how it functions is planting the seeds of Communism; but if they do not know what Communism is and how it functions, they are also planting the seeds of Communism. Mankind is currently waging an ideological war, and any general, colonel, or captain who does not know how to command ought to be demoted to the rank of corporal. And not knowing how to command includes being unable to distinguish friend from foe among the fighters, to determine whether he ought to fire on the enemy troops or if he ought to fire on his own.

There was a U.S. journalist, no less than a Pulitzer Prize

winner, who dedicated all his energies to calling the government headed by me Communist. For seven months, he devoted his life to the task of destroying a democracy. He went so far as to say that CIDES (Centro Interamericano de Estudios Sociales, or Inter-American Center for Social Studies), an institution established expressly to mold the democratic consciousness in the Dominican Republic—of which I shall speak at greater length because it was an important experiment—had trained no fewer than 17,000 Communist guerrillas. But even after the government was overthrown, the Armed Forces and the Dominican police were never able to produce one—or even part of one—of those 17,000 guerrillas. For whom was that Pulitzer Prize winner working? And the powerful U.S. newspaper chain that paid the newsman's salary—for whom was it working? And for whom, at this juncture in the world's history, is the man who destroys a democracy working?

Latin American democracy is inherently weak because of the weakness of the social structure in Latin American countries. But that weakness is intensified all over the hemisphere—with the exception, perhaps, of Canada, Mexico, Costa Rica, and Uruguay, but not the United States—by a systematic propagation of the fear of Communism without an explanation of just what Communism is. An artificial fear has been created, so diffuse and vague that people can identify it with anything that displeases them or conflicts with their desires. Communism can be anything, and anything can be Communist—a government, a book, a song, a political party, and sometimes a democratic regime rightfully established under the law. This fear has been generated deliberately: "Fear protects the orchard." The explanation of the differences between Communism and democracy is deliberately withheld from the people, because if they were explained, the common people might realize that under a democratic system they would enjoy comforts and benefits that today are appropriated by their exploiters.

Every day, accusations of Communism thunder from the newspapers and magazines, the radio and television, in conversations and coffee-hour gossip, from the pulpit. They are catapulted against any politician or intellectual who dares to preach the least reform. Such accusations create a false public opinion limited to the country's ruling groups. But though this opinion is false—because it represents a minority view—it is sufficient to justify a destructive assault on democracy and, above all, to justify the persecution of any politician or intellectual who desires a change in the people's social conditions. Such accusations, reiterated in a constant barrage everywhere and in every way, have led to the creation of a fanatic movement reminiscent in character of Savonarola's ardor or Hitler's madness. Being a democrat does not consist of just preaching democracy or living under its principles or even helping to construct a democracy. In the Dominican Republic, at least, in order to prove that I was a democrat, I would have had to follow Trujillo's old pattern: imprison, deport, or kill anyone accused of being a Communist. I would, furthermore, have had to abide by the judgment of any old general or colonel whom God had given the special gift of knowing who was and who was not a Communist. I, for example, who had never had the slightest flirtation with Communism, was a confirmed Red to some of those military men and Catholic priests.

Intense fear of Communism creates Communists. In general, fear is the worst counselor, as it leaves no room for counsel; it is cool judgment that enables one to find the best solution to any problem.

When Fidel Castro, on December 2, 1961, said that Cuba was a socialist country and that he had always been a Communist, he spoke the truth in the first instance but not in the second. Fidel had not always been a Marxist-Leninist. Perhaps he sought to justify himself to himself and to history by portraying himself as a man who had embraced an idea and remained loyal to it although he had had to practice deception. The leader of the Cuban revolution is a complex personality, and it would be difficult to pinpoint his exact reasons for making a given statement. But if we confine our attention to the consequences of what he has done and said, we find that the second part of his statement has had destructive results. The moment he said that he had always been a Marxist-Leninist—or a Communist, for in this case, they are equivalent—anyone who had ever fought for a reform democracy became a potential Communist. And being a potential Communist amounts to being a Communist in fact, to the vested political interests in the Americas.

With this declaration, Fidel Castro, who had been the leader of a fervently popular democratic revolution, engraved in red one single word, "Communist," on every attempt to make a democratic revolution for a long time to come. It is hazardous to say whether he did so consciously or unconsciously, but there can be no doubt that by doing so he rendered an incalculable service to the cause of world Communism, since after his declaration, it became virtually and even totally impossible to make a democratic revolution in this part of the world, and without a democratic revolution in Latin America, there is no way out. The Latin American revolution which is inevitable, even if it takes fifteen, twenty, or twenty-five years, should not be Communist, but the fear of the democratic revolution will make it sooner or later fall into the pattern of a Communist revolution.

The explanation that I give here applies to my case and to Angel Miolán's. We had dedicated a quarter of a century to fighting for democracy, but since we had proposed

that the Dominican democracy that was to arise after Trujillo's fall should be a reformist, revolutionary democracy—
in order to avoid perpetuating the economic, political, and
social evils that had made Trujillo's dictatorship possible—
we were accused of being Communists as soon as it became
apparent that our party was going to win the 1962 elections. Miolán and I—as leaders of the PRD, not as individuals—were going to achieve power by the democratic
route, through open and honest balloting. But in spite of
this, we were called Communists. I leave it to the reader
to imagine what accusations would have been hurled at us
if, instead of organizing a political party to launch us in
the electoral fight, we had taken the road of armed insur-
rection in order to establish democracy.

Anyone who does not demonstrate in a satisfactory manner that he respects and will continue to respect the established order in Latin America, that he will not touch a
single hair on the head of the vested interests, and that, on
the contrary, he will dedicate himself to defending them
with body and soul, night and day, is transmuted into and
suspected of being a secret Communist. A chorus of voices
all over the continent accuses him of being an agent of
Moscow and of Fidel Castro. The pressure raised everywhere in response to this accusation is of such a defamatory
nature that few can suffer it calmly. But there is an answer
to this accusation: When the youth of Latin America become indignant at the injustice committed against honest
democratic leaders, they react by shifting toward Communism. If the accusation comes from the most hated circles in the hemisphere, the youth respond to it by taking
a position against the accusers at precisely the opposite extreme. And so, day after day, the most audacious young
people in Latin America, led by those from the upper and
middle strata of the middle class, have been swelling the
Communist ranks in all our countries.

Fidel Castro has not always been a Communist, although he claims the contrary and in spite of the propaganda spawned by his adversaries, who want to hold him responsible even for events that took place when he was a schoolboy. Until 1957, Castro was a democratic revolutionary, though with somewhat confused notions of what the term meant. It is relatively clear that Castro began leaning toward Communism near the end of 1957, when he was in the Sierra Maestra. This is revealed by the letter that he wrote at that time to the Revolutionary Junta in Miami. But if, when he came out of the mountains in January, 1959, he thought that it was feasible to establish a Communist regime in Cuba, he was still not a confirmed Communist. The assumption that he favored a Communist regime as opposed to a democratic socialist set-up is based on the following observation: Castro took no measures that he would have to amend or revoke later if he established Communism. Many of his acts were indispensable to either a democratic or a Communist revolution. But there were a series of steps that were indispensable if the revolution was to be democratic, and these steps Castro did not take.

At the beginning of 1959, my family was living in Cuba and I was in Venezuela, where I had had to take refuge in April, 1958. The family asked me to come back to Cuba, but I had been observing the Castro revolution, and I did not see it giving proof of being a democratic revolution, the sort of revolution for which the great masses of South America had been waiting. In March, when the revolution had been in power less than three months, I told the family not to wait for me in Cuba, but to move to Venezuela.

It is not possible to maintain a democracy without democratic supporters. In Cuba, the creole bourgeoisie and the middle class—especially its middle and upper strata—as well as a large part of the masses, had lived for twelve years under a democratic regime and had learned nothing of democracy. They did not prize its benefits or defend it from its enemies. Beginning in 1940, despite many weaknesses in the country's moral order but few in other aspects, Cubans did live under a democracy. Nevertheless, when the democratic regime was toppled by Batista in March, 1952, the people reacted with glacial indifference. No one came forth to defend democracy. No one had any difficulty in accepting the military take-over that placed Batista in power, even though the Cubans knew that Batista had been a dictator, and a tough one, at least from 1934 to 1940. In time, a small sector of the middle stratum, and a larger group of the lower stratum, of the middle class rebelled; none of the proletariat joined them. The fruit of that uprising was Castro's revolution. In 1963, an estimated 250,000 Cubans were in exile. If that many Cubans had defended their democracy in 1952, when Batista moved to destroy it, his regime would not have lasted a week, and Castro's revolution would never have come about.

Those who do not know what a democracy is and how it functions, also do not know what Communism is and how it functions. At best, they do not know because they are unthinking or irresponsible, or because they do not understand that the political system under which a society lives is as vital to each member as the air he breathes. But often these people feign ignorance because they find such an attitude to their advantage in securing privileges and positions. In short, they close their eyes to the people in order to rob them more easily.

xiv

The Alliance for Progress

When U.S. newsmen asked me what I thought of the Alliance for Progress, I answered, in a typically Talmudic manner, with another question: "Can you tell me what the Alliance is and how it operates?" None of them could answer me, and what is worse, I never found a single U.S. official in the Dominican Republic who could answer that question, either.

Supposedly, the Alliance for Progress administers U.S. funds allotted for the development of Latin American countries, and supposedly, these funds are to be employed only in productive areas, such as education, communications, and health. But supposedly, there are also funds, available from the Inter-American Development Bank, for the construction of public housing and for loans to private industry. In the Dominican Republic, a free food-distribution service administered by two institutions, CARITAS and CARE, also came under Alliance jurisdiction.

But how, in actual fact, did the Alliance function? What procedures had to be followed in order to obtain funds?

This was some kind of jealously guarded secret. Neither Dominicans nor Americans seemed to know the answer.

What I have just said may seem cynical, but the fact is that I, the President-elect of a Latin American republic, could find no one to explain the workings of the Alliance to me. The Alliance was really a useful plan, designed to promote hemispheric development, and everyone in both the Americas should have understood how it functioned. But if I could not find out, what could be expected of the masses?

Much was said all over the hemisphere about the Alliance and the benefits that it was pouring forth; yet no one fully understood the mechanics of the plan. Consequently, all the Dominicans, especially those in the middle and upper strata of the middle class, expected it to produce miracles. Predictably, since no one quite knew how those miracles would come about or what were the limits of the resources of the plan, no one would be satisfied with the results.

To people not versed in the problems of economics and politics, like those in the elite, the ideas back of the Alliance appeared to be very simple: "The United States is the richest country in the world. Americans have millions and millions of surplus dollars, and they are going to give them to us. For them, money grows on trees anyway."

The Alliance produced a reaction that was the reverse of the reaction produced by Communism. Communism was something very bad that would take away our wealth; the Alliance was something very good that would make us rich. Everything evil was anticipated of the one, and everything good of the other. As in the Middle Ages, when each man's life depended on a saint to protect him— Goodness—in order to keep him from being claimed by the devil—Evil—for the middle and upper strata of the middle class in the Dominican Republic, there seemed to be only one path to happiness—the Alliance. The alternative was the road to disaster—Communism. A third avenue, one's own efforts carried out in a democratic atmosphere, did not exist for this sector of Dominican society, but it is this avenue that is the true, secure, and solid one. No nation was ever saved by gifts or by fear.

The Alliance for Progress constituted a help, an excellent help, which we should have received with dignity and with the realization that it was only a temporary aid measure, not a permanent crutch. This aid was intended to impel us to develop our own resources, *for the purpose of constructing a just democracy,* and to promote the general welfare. It was not, nor could it be, a flood of dollars to enrich a select few. Still less, was it a bribe to buy off our hearts and souls so that instead of creating a democracy, we would dedicate ourselves, as Trujillo had done, to hunting down real or imaginary Communists. The Alliance was intended not for buying slaves but for freeing the people from misery and dictatorship, from ignorance and sickness —provided these people wanted to free themselves from these afflictions.

The Alliance did not pour out dollars but distributed merchandise and industrial products under short- and long-term agreements. Once they reached the Dominican Republic, these goods and products were converted into Dominican pesos, which the Dominican Government and the Alliance mission utilized in specific projects. For us, the money became dollars on hand since the Central Bank did not have to draw on foreign exchange for these imports. In the long run, it did represent dollars, because it would have to be repaid in dollars seven, ten, or twelve years hence.

Here is an example: During Trujillo's regime, the United States had frozen $22,750,000 owed for Dominican sugar sold in the U.S. After Trujillo's demise, the Kennedy

Administration agreed to return that money to the Dominican Republic, not in cold cash, but through the Alliance for Progress. This meant that Dominican business would have available the equivalent value in merchandise and industrial products, including machinery and other types of capital goods. In this particular instance, the Dominican Republic would not have to repay the money in dollars after two, five, or twenty years because the funds involved were a debt that the United States owed to the Dominicans.

Now, how long would it take Dominican businessmen to purchase U.S. products in the amount of $22,750,000? They might use up their credit in six months, or they might drag the matter out for two years. Not all Dominican importers wanted to make purchases through the Alliance, because these involved restrictions that many Dominican businessmen were not disposed to comply with. For example, Alliance specifications made it impossible to evade foreign-exchange controls with crooked invoicing, a fairly common practice in the Republic. If a Dominican businessman purchased $25,000 worth of goods from the U.S., he would obtain from the U.S. exporter an invoice made out for $30,000, and deposit the $5,000 difference in a U.S. bank in an account in his name, or his wife's, or a trusted friend's. Through this practice, tens of millions of Dominican dollars piled up in the United States, when they could have been employed in the country's development instead, or added to its foreign-exchange reserve to be applied toward purchases in other countries. Also, many articles fell outside the Alliance specifications, and so had to be purchased through other channels.

Thus, there were limitations that imposed a certain rhythm on imports covered by the Alliance. The end result of all this was that it was impossible to predict over-all import figures. The Dominican Government did not know, and could not know, how long it would take to dispose of the $22,750,000. And so it was impossible for the government to set up an expense budget based on Alliance imports. One month, $200,000 worth of goods might enter the country, and the next only $100,000. With such fluctuating expenditures no sensible budget was feasible.

I should explain that the Dominican Government was to receive the equivalent amount in pesos, not U.S. dollars. In normal trade outside Alliance jurisdiction, the Dominican importer paid for his U.S. purchases in Dominican pesos deposited in any of the Republic's recognized banks —specifically, the bank through which the U.S. exporter operated. This bank then exchanged the pesos for dollars at the Central Bank, and drew a dollar draft credited to the U.S. firm. But in Alliance transactions, the Dominican importer paid a local bank, which delivered the money to the Central Bank, which in turn deposited it in a special account at the disposal of the Alliance mission in Santo Domingo.

That money was to be used for Alliance projects in the Dominican Republic. Those projects were planned and executed through government channels, at least during my administration, although with the advice and guidance of the Alliance mission.

Obviously, the mechanics of the Alliance for Progress were not so difficult to explain. The same system operated in every country in Latin America. This was not the mystery of the seven veils. Why, then, were they not explained to the Dominicans and to the Americans? I discovered the reason in Washington, and not because it was explained to me, but as a result of talks with the Coordinator of the Alliance, Teodoro Moscoso, and with the head of the Alliance mission in the Dominican Republic, Newell F. Williams. On this occasion, the Kennedy Administration had just promised the government I had been elected to head that the

United States would repay the old sugar debt in dollars. At this time the Dominican Republic, itself and through the Central Bank, was saddled with more than $45 million in debts payable in dollars. The dollar reserve in the Central Bank totaled less than $8 million. I was informed that the money for the sugar compensation could not be paid in dollars under Alliance procedure.

There were two principal reasons why this procedure had been set up. The United States balance-of-payments deficit was approaching $1.5 billion a year. Although the export of industrial goods and other merchandise from the United States was, in effect, a dollar export that would increase the deficit, that increase was not entered on the books, because the U.S. Government paid exporters or guaranteed payment for the goods. However, in an effort to assure the success of the Alliance, the Kennedy Administration had arranged an agreement—the classic U.S. "compromise"—with financial institutions in the United States, whereby U.S. dollars would leave the country not in cash but in agricultural or industrial goods.

For the Dominican Republic, which had been stripped of all its capital by the Trujillo family, Alliance aid was important, indeed imperative. But it was not enough. The country was in a volatile state. The world around us had undergone transformation, and that transformation had produced new social problems, as well as benefits. We were being affected by the problems, but not by the benefits.

Before initiating any project requiring Alliance funds, the constitutional government had to wait until sufficient funds were accumulated to cover the expenditures anticipated. For example, if a school costing 1 million pesos was projected, the government had to hold up the start of construction until 400,000 or 500,000 pesos had mounted up, since we could not put architects, builders, foremen, bricklayers, carpenters, and laborers to work if a month or two later we would have to suspend operations for lack of funds.

And we had great projects ahead of us, works necessary if we planned to advance production at the hoped-for rate so as to achieve in a few years the consumption level required by a thriving population with an annual growth rate of more than 3 per cent. Fundamentally, we needed road networks linking rural areas with consumption centers; we needed docks, dams, canals, and electricity. The production of electricity was so low that in June, 1963, it was absolutely impossible to increase electric consumption by a single light bulb per home.

Every sociology student knows that in any country the bureaucratic organization tends toward a centralization of authority that can lead to increasing centralization of activity. This tendency is much more pronounced when the organization is international, but no one in that kind of organization can remain immune to the hunger for power and the resulting necessity to centralize activities. Many sociologists have tried to explain the cause of this tendency. It seems clear that it originates in the fear felt by each individual in the group that he will lose his position if the group does not engage in activities that ostensibly justify its existence.

In the international order, there is a group of agencies that compete among themselves in great works intended to stimulate the development of poor countries. These agencies range from the World Bank to the Inter-American Development Bank, from the United Nations to the Organization of American States. All employ high-salaried technicians with liberal travel accounts. Unquestionably, some of them believe passionately in their work and are rendering an important service to humanity. But there can be no doubt that many of them unconsciously further the law of increasing centralization of activities that governs the bodies that employ them.

A characteristic result of this is that many of these international agencies want to sponsor projects in a poor country at the same time. Naturally, these projects have to be studied carefully and without haste, from all angles except the one that really matters in a truly backward country— the need for urgency.

When Jacob Javits, the Republican Senator from New York, discussed this facet of development problems with me, I became convinced that the Dominican Republic needed—in addition to the Alliance, which was of great help in dealing with everyday problems—substantial investments in various large-scale projects that only private sources could fund. I went to Europe in January, 1963, and reached an agreement in principle with a Swiss consortium. It was to provide $150 million in projects for the Dominican Republic, of which the government would repay $15 million in the first two years—$7.5 million a year—but only after that money had been invested in the Republic. The balance would be repaid twelve years later. All expenditures made in Dominican territory would be paid for in dollars, which the Swiss group would bring into the country. Work on the projects and costs would be supervised by a bureau created for that purpose by the Dominican Government, along with a qualified foreign firm. As the studies by the Dominican Government were insufficient to commit the entire $150 million, the project would begin with works accounting for $90 million: two major dams, each with a hydroelectric installation and canal network; a thermoelectric plant; an expanded aqueduct for the capital. Meanwhile, further studies would investigate the best application for the remaining $60 million.

This contract, to be carried out by General Electric of England, raised the Dominican Republic's international credit and thereby unleased a wave of international offers. Suddenly dozens and dozens of consortia and construction companies appeared on the scene, though previously they had never wasted a glance at the little Antilles nation. They were all interested in the contract or in others like it. Of course, this agreement also set off a wave of criticism from the international agencies, lamenting the fact that the Dominican Republic had to pay open-market interest rates, when it could have achieved the same by paying international-agency rates. Naturally, leaders of the political *ventorrillos* placed themselves at the service of the competitors of British General Electric. After the constitutional administration was overthrown, the contract was canceled, although the new government was unable to present a single argument to justify this.

Needless to say, Latin American oligarchies that opposed the Alliance for Progress because it demanded social and economic reforms were happy to enlist the opinions of the international agencies when it suited their purposes. If one of those agencies stated that private funds should not be used for development works because the interest rates were too high, the oligarchy raged against using these funds. With admirable flexibility, these Latin leaders changed form and color several times a day, took advantage of whatever served their purposes, upset the best plans, seized on the parts that fitted the circumstances, and always managed to come out with the lion's share.

The Alliance for Progress was evil, according to those circles, because it demanded agrarian and fiscal reforms. But when the Dominican Government tried to accomplish outside the Alliance something that would produce a change in the country's economic structure, the oligarchy sallied forth, like an impartial knight-errant to proclaim that the Alliance was the only source of help.

The result was that the Alliance proved to be neither

good nor evil. It was simply a useful tool, the type of aid that could have helped to prevent many ills Latin America had long endured, had it been inaugurated in time—that is, before World War II precipitated the formation in these countries of a financial and industrial oligarchy with the mentality of a *latifundista*. The Alliance was neither good nor bad in itself because it was vitally dependent on how the aid was administered. Where Alliance funds were properly and honestly managed, to further the development of the country, not the political advantage of the ruling party or the personal benefit of members of the oligarchy, the Alliance was good. Where it was administered corruptly, for political purposes, or to satisfy the appetites of a single group, it was bad. But where the Alliance became a propaganda mechanism for the glorification of the United States or any Latin government enjoying its benefits, it was neither good nor bad, but useless. Political capital should not be made out of Latin America's tragedy.

The shortcomings of the Alliance were not inherent in it. They were born of the Latin American character, and were our historical shortcomings. The manner in which Alliance funds were applied led to negative results, which my administration tried to avoid, and I believe that we succeeded to a great extent. But the Dominican constitutional government had the avowed intention of achieving reforms in every field, not excluding the moral, and it, therefore, used Alliance aid to serve the people, not persons or groups.

However, we must not forget that any democratic Latin American government that refuses to use its power for the benefit of the chosen few, either nations or foreigners, cannot survive in this underdeveloped world of pirates with Cadillacs. Such a government must be a Communist regime and must forthwith be smashed.

The Men of the Alliance

Latin American democracy has many enemies, and undoubtedly the most powerful of them are inside Latin America—the intrinsic weakness of its social structures and the lack of self-respect, of love of country, and of faith in the future. But few of these enemies cause such immediate damage as irresponsible U.S. newspapermen. There are responsible ones, but I am speaking of those who are not.

To become experts on Latin America requires little effort by U.S. newsmen—so little, in fact, that few of them take the trouble to learn Spanish. It seems to suffice that one day, for one reason or another, they run into a politician from this part of the world and hear his views on hemispheric problems. Or possibly a U.S. newsman finds himself on vacation in a Latin American country when some incident occurs. His paper assigns him to cover it, and he is launched on his career as an expert.

As for the Alliance for Progress, every U.S. correspondent that passed through the Dominican Republic on his return to the United States wrote an article that followed the same pattern. Invariably, the Alliance was accomplishing all the good coming out of the new constitutional government, and the Dominican administration was making all the mistakes.

This practice was deceitful, humiliating, and dangerous. My administration held office for only seven months less two days. In seven months, no constitutional government can accomplish anything worthwhile. A revolutionary government—not required to act in legislative matters through a congress, not obliged to plan slowly and carefully—that rules by decree can do a lot in that time. But my administration found itself without a single study of any problem, the government budget already in its third month and faced with a serious deficit, and the currency situation at a crisis. The first year of my government was intended to be a period of adjustment, planning, and economic shoring-up.

The PRD had won the election with the vote of the poorest masses. The middle and upper strata of the middle class and a sizable portion of the lower stratum had cast their votes for other parties. On coming to power, the constitutional government began adjusting the budget by lowering the salaries of its personnel. The monthly compensation of ministers dropped from $2,000 to $1,000, of a deputy minister, from $900 to $700. The salaries of ambassadors, embassy secretaries, and other foreign-service officers were reduced by even greater percentages. Some diplomatic officials had been earning more than $5,000 a month, a crime in a country where people are dying of hunger. There were men collecting salaries of $1,000 a month without ever showing up for work. The salary cutbacks in the state bureaucracy affected principally the middle class, as class limits in the Dominican Republic are relative to the economy of the country. Anyone earning

600 pesos a month is a member of the middle stratum. An Ambassador belongs to the upper stratum.

The two upper strata had been the PRD's adversaries, and in the Dominican Republic, an adversary is an enemy to the death. When people in these strata, which influenced the Armed Forces and the priesthood and at the same time were influenced by them, read articles in the U.S. press or translations of them, eulogizing only the accomplishments of the Alliance, they became increasingly more inclined to regard the Dominican Government as a crew of incompetents. In short, they felt that the United States Government was helping their sworn enemy, which made them unreasonably anti-U.S.

At the same time, Dominican officials who were working sixteen hours a day to lay the foundations of a democratic system of government felt humiliated by U.S. newspaper articles that quite plainly ignored their efforts. They reacted by taking a stand gradually and almost unconsciously in opposition to both the United States and the Alliance for Progress.

A matter so delicate as the foreign relations of a country with worldwide interests, such as the United States, should not, and cannot, be left to the mercy of unqualified and irresponsible newsmen. Some of these journalists are frankly enemies of Latin American democracy, and few understand the political undercurrents of Latin America.

Today's U.S. citizens are not faced with the almost heroic, and certainly very honorable, task of creating a democracy. They found theirs made when they came into the world. They do not know or even imagine what effort it costs, how much labor it demands, how much passion it requires, to undertake the task of creating a democracy at precisely the time when democracy has more enemies and faces more dangers than ever before. The U.S. citizen today has only to defend the privileges that he enjoys under a democratic regime. But the defense of these privileges so obsesses him that he thinks that every other nation ought to dedicate itself to defending them for him. He fails to understand that other nations also want these privileges and benefits, and have to begin by establishing a democracy. They cannot defend what does not exist. For Latin Americans, this is not the time to fight for U.S. democracy, but rather the time to create their own.

The average U.S. newsman's attitude toward Latin American events is mortifying for anyone involved in creating a system of government that can achieve development without infringing individual liberty. Usually the approach is frivolous; sometimes it maligns; almost always it is downright ignorant. Worst of all, these newsmen do not know that by harming Latin American democracy they are endangering U.S. democracy—and along with it, the benefits that enable them to travel on lavish expense accounts throughout Latin America, writing the critiques their readers feed on.

The damage inflicted by such irresponsible journalism is incalculable. The day that a wreath must be placed on the tomb of what could have been Latin American democracy, the time will have come when the United States must bury its own democracy.

Alliance for Progress projects were already well under way when the constitutional government took office on February 27, 1963. Although Newell Williams, the Alliance mission head in the Dominican Republic, informed me that the plans could be adapted to suit the new regime, there was no thought of leaving the projects half-finished. Williams was really the right man to head the mission. He was born in Colombia, had lived in Paraguay, spoke Spanish with a Costa Rican accent, and was truly interested in helping the Dominican Republic.

There were several obstacles to bringing Alliance projects into being in the Dominican Republic. To begin with, there was a shortage of capable technical personnel. What the Trujillo dictatorship had done in the area of technical training was criminal. When studies by the constitutional government had progressed far enough for us to calculate which projects would be under way by February, 1964, we realized we would have to import engineers. The number in our country was clearly inadequate for the task at hand. When we looked for agronomists and veterinarians, we were informed that we had fewer than twenty-five men in each of these fields. As quickly as possible, we sent abroad students or young professionals to acquire at top speed a specialty of their choice. There was everything to be done and no one to do it.

The U.S. technical experts sent in to help us—with the exception of the young people in the Peace Corps—were simply not suited to the job at hand. U.S. technical know-how is very expensive, and we had to pay these people with money that should have been applied to our public-works projects. A U.S. expert is geared to work in an expensive environment. If he is in Massachusetts and needs information from San Francisco, he simply picks up the telephone and calls long distance. The following day he gets a 3,000-word telegram containing detailed information, complete down to the last comma. We needed cheaper technical assistance. Furthermore, U.S. technicians frequently did not even know the language, much less the psychology, history, and social composition of the Dominican people.

We got our best results from Latin American experts, including Puerto Ricans. The Puerto Rican Government gave us every possible support in this. The so-called troika —the OAS, the U.N. Economic Commission for Latin America (Comisión Económica para América Latina), and the Inter-American Development Bank—sent in a mission, which was just starting work when my government was toppled. I requested that the mission begin by organizing a bureau of the budget and preparing Dominican specialists in this field. We were still using an antiquated system dating from the first years of the U.S. occupation, 1916–24, and although the Director was a capable and honest man, he was enmeshed in a system that could not adapt to the modern concept of a budget as an instrument of development.

There was another negative side to the Alliance—hordes suddenly appeared to fish in its river of dollars. Every day brought two or three new proposals for public-works projects under the Alliance. Sometimes Alliance funds were simply spent for no useful purpose. During the rule of the Council of State, a firm made a study of agrarian reform and for its efforts charged a small fortune—$250,000. The study could never have served as even the initial step in a planned reform. At the cost of $100,000, another firm made a study of governmental organization that could have been written by a boy of fourteen lost in utopian daydreams.

The country's lack of a stable bureaucracy made the government's work all the harder. I have already explained the negative attitudes of the middle class, and with such people, who had no sense of loyalty to anything, it would take years to establish a responsible civil service.

Finally, the Alliance wanted to do everything at once: build roads, schools, aqueducts, and hospitals; train teachers; develop agriculture; construct bridges and public housing. Consequently, funds were spread so thin that there was too little money for each undertaking. Thus, agrarian reform was hindered and schools were built too slowly. On taking office, the constitutional government found a host of projects under way that could not be halted. Both the Alliance and the Dominican Republic would have gained a great deal if their major efforts had been concentrated in two or three key areas—education, agricultural development, a road network, for example. In the first two, limiting the effort to certain clearly defined aims might have answered our needs still better, perhaps to building schools and training teachers in the former instance, and to extending credits and preparing experts on specific crops in the latter.

Newell Williams and Ambassador Martin were eager to help the Republic, and the White House responded with enthusiasm to any suggestion from either of them.

In truth, Martin and Williams did not appear to be agents of the U.S. Government but rather two Dominicans as anxious as the best of Dominicans to accomplish the impossible for us. They were anything but coldblooded officials looking out only for the interests of their own country and government. Williams had an unending flow of ideas. He tracked me down everywhere, at home, in the National Palace, day or night, with the most unexpected proposals. All were designed to benefit the little, weak Dominican Republic. If I accepted a plan of his, he ran to Martin to begin work on it as soon as possible. Many serious problems requiring difficult solutions were resolved by these two within twenty-four hours.

And dealing with me was no easy matter. I am fully aware of that. I was very sensitive to anything that might affect Dominican sovereignty. My poor country had had, from the first breath of its life as a republic, a string of political leaders who had dedicated all their skills and resources to looking for any foreign power on which to unload our independence. We Dominicans were born as a Colombian protectorate in Bolívar's time. Later we formed part of Haiti's territory, until 1844. After seventeen years as a republic, we went back to being a Spanish colony, in 1861—at our own request, not at Spain's instigation. In 1870, we did everything in our power to deliver the country to the United States. And at the end of the last century, we again suggested becoming a U.S. protectorate.

I felt wounded, as if it were a personal affront, at the spectacle of so many men without faith in the destiny of their own country. In my childhood, I had seen the Dominican flag coming down from the public buildings to give way to the U.S. banner. No one will ever know what my seven-year-old soul suffered at the sight. I cannot imagine how ballads about Mexico's Pancho Villa reached La Vega, the tiny town in which I was born and reared, but when I heard how he had stood up against American soldiers invading Mexico, he became my idol. I probably knew nothing in those days of the founders of the Dominican Republic, Duarte and Sánchez and Mella. But I knew enough of Martí, of Máximo Gómez, of Maceo, and I sang the songs of the Cuban war. This probably explains why Pancho Villa became for me the sum and symbol of all the Cuban heroes. At night I prayed for the appearance of a Dominican Pancho Villa, someone who would do in our country what Pancho Villa had done in Mexico and what Martí, Gómez, and Maceo had done in Cuba.

The man of today was foreshadowed in yesterday's child. Perhaps I love my little Antilles country so passionately because when I became aware of it as a nation, I realized that it was not that at all, but a dominion. This caused me indescribable pain, and often kept me awake a long time after I had been sent to bed, even though it is difficult for a child to stay awake. By the time I was ten, I was ashamed that Santana, who annexed the country to Spain in 1863, and Báez, who wanted to turn Samana over to the United States, were Dominicans. As the years passed, that pain and that shame became transformed into passionate patriotism. When I began writing, it was with the same passion. When it fell to me to be the leader of a political party and the President of my country, I was very careful always to conduct myself as a Dominican who was proud of his nationality.

Martin and Williams always respected my national pride. They never gave the impression that they were extending charity to the Dominican people. They never made me feel that they represented the most powerful government in the world. They displayed exemplary tact, and a humility that is difficult for people who know they are strong.

Behind them, across the sea, was a man with inspirational qualities. It was he who conceived the Alliance for Progress—John Fitzgerald Kennedy.

There have been four moments in American history when the United States gave off a brilliance that shed warmth on the downtrodden people of the earth, and especially those of Latin America. One of these moments took place in the eighteenth century when the U.S. democracy was created, when Thomas Paine, Benjamin Franklin, and George Washington represented the most radical ideals of humanity. Another came with the freeing of the slaves in the nineteenth century, when the name of Abraham Lincoln was blessed by the Negroes and the oppressed of the continent. A third was the era of the New Deal, when Roosevelt confronted the giants of Wall Street and proved to be the champion of the common man in every nation. And finally there was the brief and impassioned hour of history that was John F. Kennedy's. Of those four moments, the one most directly touching the Latin American heart was that embodied by Kennedy.

The Alliance for Progress may or may not have been good; it may or may not have been useful. It had positive and negative facets; every human effort is filled with weaknesses and strengths. But the Alliance for Progress was created with the unmistakable goal of accelerating the political, economic, and social development of Latin America. If the Alliance benefited the United States, that was only fair. Every leader in any country thinks of the interests of his country, and it is his duty to protect them. But there is a difference—a decided difference—between the "big stick" of Theodore Roosevelt and the Alliance for Progress. Roosevelt acted for the United States, without any concern for the interests of either Panama or Colombia, when he ordered the construction of the canal. Kennedy acted in the interests of the United States when he proposed the Alliance for Progress, but he was also thinking of the destiny of democracy in Latin America.

When I met with Kennedy in the White House at the beginning of January, 1963, I carefully observed the young man—too young, perhaps, to be President of the most powerful nation in the world—and I watched him while I spoke and while he talked to me. He was dressed simply—not soberly, but simply: light-brown shoes, gray suit with a white pinstripe, blue tie, white shirt; all his clothing had been worn, none of it was new—as if in an effort to avoid offending Dominican poverty with an exhibition of American wealth. He acted with the naturalness of an old friend. We reviewed problems common to our two countries. When I told him that the Dominicans were hungry, he was moved as if he had been wounded. We looked each other in the eye. I told him that the Council of State, almost *sub rosa,* had granted an oil-refinery concession to a well-known U.S. firm on terms reminiscent of the days of his country's most flagrant imperialism, and that I was going to rescind that contract. When I mentioned the word imperialism, I saw the pain in his face. "That is a delicate point, but we will help you," he said. Some months later, the powerful company renounced the contract.

From that and other points in our conversation, I deduced that Kennedy felt that he, and only he, was responsible for his country's errors in Latin America in every era, from the time of George Washington right down to the days of Dwight Eisenhower. Here was the affecting case of a statesman with the sensibility of a mystic, perhaps resulting from his Irish origin and his Catholic faith. Was it his sense of guilt for the wrongs that his countrymen had perpetrated, and a resolve to right these wrongs, that prompted him to act as a reformer beyond the borders of his own country? Perhaps. In any case, a mystic with the mind and body of a top-level politician is rare in human history. I could understand his feeling; I took as a personal affront the attitude of Dominicans who had sold out their country. And perhaps that emotion, which I had borne over the years, enabled me to perceive what was going on in Kennedy's soul.

Such a man did not differentiate between the underprivileged and the exploited Latin American and the U.S. Negro mistreated and segregated in his own country. Having the capacity to suffer for others, he could not as a leader limit himself to the problems and interests of the country he governed. He would necessarily be a man of conscience pained by the humiliation of any man anywhere.

The day I ascended to the presidency, Kennedy sent me a gift, delivered by his personal representative at the inaugural ceremony, Vice President Lyndon B. Johnson. It was not something for my personal use; it was an ambulance for the Dominican people. This tells more about Kennedy than I can.

John Fitzgerald Kennedy was felled by an assassin's bullet. Although the machinery of the Alliance for Progress survived him, the vitality and spirit of reform with which he imbued it when he created it, died with him in Dallas on November 22, 1963. And so I have written about the Alliance for Progress in the past tense.

CIDES—An Important Experiment

When this book speaks of middle-class youth, it does so with the purpose of putting a certain group of young people within a social context. Thereby their level of culture, their kind of sensitivity, their concerns should all come into focus. But "middle-class youth" in the Dominican Republic does not quite conform to the psychology of the country's middle-class as a whole. As in any other part of the world, middle-class young people in the Dominican Republic are idealists. They have a scale of social values that they defend stubbornly. And they love their country.

This has always been the case. The founders of the Republic—Duarte, Sánchez, and Mella—were almost children when they secretly organized La Trinitaria to liberate the country from Haiti. Luperón was barely more than an adolescent when the war of restoration broke out in 1863. Gregorio Urbano Gilbert had the faint beginnings of down on his face when he fired his revolver against the American Marines at San Pedro de Macorís in 1916.

In 1962, middle-class Dominican youth had been propagating fierce patriotism, and as I have explained, that feeling tended to be anti-American. I had to be careful in dealing with these spirited youth. If there was ever to be democracy in the Dominican Republic, these boys and girls would have to support and defend it. The middle class to which their parents belonged had been damaged to its core by the vices of the Trujillo dictatorship. It was now incapable of creative labor and of anything requiring common effort.

Any possible Dominican democracy, then, must be a labor of the future, not the past. The past was infamy, and nothing of worth could be extracted from it. Therefore, from the outset the seeds of the future must be sown with strength of will and an all-or-nothing spirit. The democracy due to be born in the Dominican Republic on February 27, 1963, must be pure in its respect for all forms of liberty, even for excesses in the use of those liberties. It must be pure in its management of public funds, which would require each high official to watch for corruption. It must be pure in the private life of its officials. It must be pure and firm in its treatment of reactionary forces both within and outside the country. It must be pure in its relations with other countries, especially the United States. A democracy so conceived might survive six months or a year, but its memory would persist to light all of Dominican history, an achievement once attained could be attained again sometime in the future.

For Dominican young people who had learned under Trujillo to hate anything called democracy—the term applied to his regime by the dictator and by politicians and the foreign press, especially the U.S. press, which called him the great democratic leader of Latin America—it was essential to create a model of the perfect democracy, to the extent that mortal man can achieve anything perfect. It must be an honest democracy, productive and sober. This was the least they would expect. And if no one gave them such a model, there would be no hope for democracy in the Dominican future.

For help with this task from the United States, my administration could count on two organizations: the Peace Corps and the Inter-American Center for Social Studies (CIDES). The Peace Corps is well known: U.S. boys and girls who scattered throughout a nation to join the humble people and work side by side with them to teach them better solutions to the immediate problems of everyday living. As an instrument of foreign policy, the Peace Corps was the most intelligent and fruitful creation of the Kennedy Administration. From a government-to-government level, it brought relations between the United States and the underdeveloped countries down to a people-to-people basis. CIDES was an experimental program of a private nature. It deserves special attention in this book, because it was an experiment that should not be forgotten.

In discussing CIDES, I must mention Norman Thomas and Sacha Volman. Thomas, the veteran American Socialist, is too well known in twentieth-century U.S. politics to repeat his story here. I will say, though, that Thomas was the very heart of the Institute of International Labor Research, for which Volman worked.

Volman was born in Bessarabia, Romania, in 1922 or 1923. His father was a wealthy man, but the son very early leaned toward Socialism. Romania had a long history of anti-Russian feeling, and this was probably especially keen in Bessarabia, which lay on the Russian border. This explains why Volman, like most of the young men of his generation, was frankly hostile to Communism. Romania had fought for centuries to obtain civil liberties, and when Volman was a boy, Stalin was ruling in Russia. The patriotic anti-Communism of Volman's childhood grew into hatred for the ruthless Stalinist dictatorship. In those days, Romania was exploited by British, French, and German corporations, which exerted a prominent influence on national affairs. These foreign firms gave their support to a regime controlled by feudal landholders and backed by the armed forces of military leaders with aristocratic origins. For that reason, Volman grew up with strongly nationalistic and anti-imperialistic feelings. These factors all combined to mold the young Volman into an ardent Socialist, who left his parents' wealthy home when he was barely fifteen to go to Bucharest, the Romanian capital, to fight for what he believed was right. He was imprisoned by the Nazis when Hitler's troops occupied the country. He escaped death at the hands of the Nazis only to become the victim of Communist persecution, when Hitler's troops were replaced by Stalin's. Volman finally fled Romania hidden in a wooden box.

This background is worth relating because the first twenty-five or twenty-eight years of Sacha Volman's life resemble those of any young Latin American fighting for the same principles. It is a story of the fight for liberty, the same struggle that has engaged generation after generation of Latin Americans since the beginning of the nineteenth century. It is, in short, the same battle to the death that we have waged in Latin America against foreign powers and their reactionary national allies. That similarity explains why, from his first contact with Latin American democratic revolutionary movements, Volman understood them completely and committed himself to helping them. With the support of Norman Thomas and Thomas' friends, he obtained funds from various foundations in order to set up the Institute of Political Education in Costa Rica, the first serious effort of its kind ever attempted in Latin America. Its aim was to mold democratic leaders with a clear ideology and sufficient awareness of what democracy is and its potential for renewed vigor.

I met Volman in 1957 and immediately realized he was more than an idealist and a man convinced that democracy could prevail against a sea of enemies. He was also a man with practical ideas who was capable of putting them into action. I worked with his Institute in Costa Rica, and it was there, as I told at the beginning of this book, that I learned that Trujillo had just been shot to death.

Shortly before the PRD delegates were to set out for the Dominican Republic, I asked Volman a favor: Would he go on ahead of them to feel out the atmosphere? If the PRD delegates arrived in Dominican territory without popular feeling to support them, the lives of all three—Miolán, Silfa, and Castillo—would be in jeopardy. Volman went. And it was love at first sight. The Dominican people captured his heart forever. From that moment on, Volman dedicated himself, heart and soul, to helping the Dominicans.

Volman's case provides a good example of what happens in Latin America. On his first trip to the country, he realized that on Trujillo's death Dominican youth would emerge from the catacombs of dictatorship full of political zeal but without any direction. He then set about organizing a special course in democratic leadership for fifty-odd Dominican young people, about half of them from the PRD, a few from the 14th of June, and the rest from the UCN. All were sent to Costa Rica for almost two months of study. On that occasion, the MPD—Marxist-Leninist-Fidelist by the definition of its own members—accused Volman of being an imperialist agent, a member of the FBI, and a host of other things I do not recall. That happened in the middle of 1961. Two years later, in the middle of 1963, when CIDES had begun to bear fruit and was obviously making a useful contribution to Dominican democracy, the factions behind the coup launched a typically cheap attack on Volman, and this time he was no FBI or imperialist agent at all, but rather an operative for Khrushchev and Castro. Thus, in two years, the same man had been a target for Communist persecution and for reactionary persecution. In two years, he had been the object of the ugliest MPD accusations and the ugliest accusations of those behind the coup. Before it was over, Volman was persecuted by the police, too. At the time of the coup, when the police searched his house, they made off with everything, including his razor and his shoes and socks, comporting themselves with the thoroughness characteristic of military *coups d'état* in Latin America.

CIDES was not administered by the Alliance for Progress, nor did it have any bureaucratic tie with the U.S. Government. In fact, it was precisely in its independent status that the organization's worth as an experiment lay. Of course, through Volman and Thomas, it maintained friendly relations with the White House and perhaps with the State Department, and I think that it once applied for Alliance aid for a particular project. But in general, to the best of my knowledge, it operated with funds received voluntarily from private American foundations.

CIDES recruited Cuban exiles, Puerto Ricans lent by their government, Venezuelans, Peruvians, Argentines, people from all over the Americas who shared a known democratic viewpoint, a desire for public service, and experienced technical skills. The Dominican Government rented CIDES a site for its headquarters and a house for Volman, for which he paid twice what the house had cost under the Council of State. CIDES also maintained a downtown office. The organization's headquarters were located at what had once been one of Ramfis Trujillo's farms, near the military base at San Isidro. Like the other farms once owned by Ramfis, this one was lavish, with many guest rooms, a swimming pool, and at least one generous barracks for a company of soldiers. The house CIDES took was called Jainamosa, and there the organization installed its field agencies, including a school.

The school taught cooperativism and Latin American political history. As President, I personally gave the lectures on the Dominican Republic. It also offered courses for schoolteachers. The students came from all over the country, with no discrimination by class or political party, so that there were PRD members as well as members of the parties that were to be behind the coup. The objective of these classes was to help create in Santo Domingo a democratic consciousness and an awareness of Dominican problems and how to go about solving them by democratic measures. CIDES was working for the country, not for any particular party.

In order to convey some picture of the extent of the coup madness, and the methods employed by its agents, I shall tell this story: Around August, 1963, the Director of National Security came to me one day with a report that had been brought in by one of his men. According to that report, which was supposedly confidential and intended to strengthen government security, the classes given by CIDES professors were teaching Communism and—I swear that the foolish charge that was later to be repeated appeared in this report—racism, too. The agent said that this information had been given him by his wife, a schoolteacher taking a course at CIDES in improved techniques. His report went on to say that films of Fidel Castro were being shown, accompanied by appropriate propaganda lectures, which declared that Castro was the revolutionary leader of Latin America, the great leader whom everyone must follow. Also, the report said, a Puerto Rican professor—whose name was given, along with an insulting comment—had told his class that the Dominican nation would never develop, because it was a country of Negroes and mulattoes; moreover, this professor had forbidden a student to sit at a table with the rest because he was not white. This report had been delivered to the Director of National Security, but without his knowledge, it had first been placed in the hands of those preparing the coup. This was nothing new. Every day similar fabrications came to their attention, and were broadcast over the radio or printed in a special publication put out just to spread such stories.

CIDES worked for months organizing a vast public-education campaign to be broadcast on television. Teachers from various countries were brought together for this program, along with specialists in educational television and in literacy programs. A Dominican teacher was sent to Puerto Rico and the United States for special training. To establish a solid foundation for the educational series, the first fifty films were devoted to instruction in reading and writing. On September 24, just fourteen hours before the coup, Volman came to see me, accompanied by an official of one of the foundations backing CIDES, because the time had come to set up the first 200 television sets and the foundation could supply only 50. The literacy program was never launched, and a few months after the coup, CIDES gave the films to the government for whatever use it might make of them.

One day, in Volman's presence, the Minister of Health complained about his department's lack of resources to combat an outbreak of polio that threatened to expand to a catastrophic epidemic. Without wasting a second, Volman mobilized all the human resources at his disposal. He flew to the United States, and—with the help of Senator Javits, the White House (and there of Ralph Dungan, particularly), a pharmaceutical firm, whose name I regrettably have forgotten, and Pan American Airways—got together 750,000 units of oral vaccine, plus 100,000 that came from

President López Mateos' government in Mexico. All of the Dominican infants were vaccinated against this dread disease. In carrying out this task, the entire country worked together, with surprising solidarity. I saw women arrive at the vaccination stations with a child in each arm and two or three more trailing behind.

This mass immunization cost the Dominican Government not a single centavo, except, of course, for the expenses of the government officials who took part in it. Everything that CIDES contributed was free.

CIDES had among its technical experts a top-level group headed by Alvin Mayne, whose experience in Puerto Rico was invaluable for a U.S. expert. He had observed Latin American psychology, its many difficulties, and the high value that it placed on subtle aspects of certain attitudes. His group was in our country to fill the gap created by the lack of Dominican technicians, until there were enough trained people to meet the government's needs.

The government had a National Planning Board, served by spirited young people who worked often until very late at night. They were neither numerous enough nor qualified enough in all matters of the science of government. The young people themselves organized their studies and made as good use of their time as they could. They got their training from experts sent to our country by international agencies, and CIDES helped them. In another two or three years, the Board would mature, but for the time being, the group of CIDES technical experts would do what it could.

I turned over to CIDES another job, a study of the laws setting import duties. There were four separate import taxes, each with a different name. A country so small and poor could not manage those taxes efficiently and honestly because of the numerous personnel required to inspect the merchandise, make all the calculations, and collect the money. When no one made a mistake, someone with sticky fingers was in the pot. CIDES undertook the study, and the reader can imagine how much effort had to be expended simply because of the circumstances: no statistics, no previous studies, no scientific basis from which to derive correct conclusions. The government's intention was to consolidate all these taxes, wait a few months while the results were analyzed, and then reorganize the entire customs system for maximum public benefit. A bill to this effect was before Congress at the time of the coup.

CIDES also worked with the National Planning Board and the Ministry of Industry and Commerce in mapping out a bill for industrial development, which I sent to Congress the day before the coup. Under the guidance of José Arroyo Riestra, on leave from the Banco de Cooperativas of Puerto Rico, CIDES had prepared two proposals. One, the General Cooperative Law, was to coordinate all future cooperative activities and those already under development. The other was to create the Institute for Cooperative Credit. The two proposed laws complemented each other, and I had sent the second to the National Monetary Board for its comments. The two bills had not yet been sent to Congress at the time of the overthrow.

The government brought to power by the coup signed all these proposals into law without adding or deleting so much as a comma, and announced them as its own work. Moreover, *Time* magazine praised a member of this government's triumvirate as the author of these laws. And so the ironical outcome was that the instigators of the coup turned to their own advantage the work of an organization that they had discredited as Communist in the cheap propaganda that they had disseminated to justify their overthrow of the constitutional government. Unfortunately, this is how the reactionaries operate in Latin America—

with a lack of regard for the truth and even for their own dignity.

CIDES was a unique experiment in Latin America. It was an agency of neither the U.S. nor the Dominican Government. It was a private foundation, supported by private funds, that worked closely with both governments. In every instance, CIDES was directed by Americans—Volman had become a U.S. citizen many years before—and served by Latin Americans and Dominicans, who were faithful to their own governments and to the Dominican, and never encountered situations that might infringe on Dominican sovereignty. It was an important experiment that should be repeated in other countries. It did at the top government level what the Peace Corps was doing at the mass level.

If CIDES had any political failing, as attacks by the reactionaries would indicate, it lay in the Dominican setting, and not in the organization itself, much less the intention with which it was created or its administrators. The Dominican Republic was not prepared to receive the benefits of CIDES. A country that had just emerged from a dictatorship as prolonged and as ruthless as Trujillo's was not politically or morally sane. CIDES would have been accepted only if it had had the authority of the U.S. Government behind it. However, had that been the case, the young people would have looked on CIDES with less receptive eyes, and it was among the young that the seeds of democracy had to be sown. The middle class, so corrupted under Trujillo, was sterile soil for democracy. In its soul grew only hatred, vulgarity, and an appetite for illicit profits. Even anti-Trujilloists, people of good faith, made the dictator their model. The image of Trujillo, rich, omnipotent, master of lives, honors, and luxurious estates, lived on as a sacred idol in these empty hearts. The principle of the replacement of the chief in primitive communities, accomplished by eating the heart or the head of a conquered chieftain, had been revived in the Dominican Republic in the second half of the twentieth century. The majority of anti-Trujillo leaders wanted to replace Trujillo, not to change the regime, and in order to destroy the democratic administration, they applied Trujillo's methods. CIDES was just one more victim of those methods.

The Conflicts with Haiti

Today Cuba is the "Pearl of the Antilles," but the name originally belonged to Hispaniola, old Santo Domingo or Saint-Domingue. The lofty rise of the mountains, the density and richness of the forests, the abundance of fresh water, the size, number, and amazing fertility of the valleys, all justify the term. A political act, however, demeaned our island in the eyes of scholars and travelers. It became divided into two separate countries, Haiti and the Dominican Republic, with two different languages, histories, and origins. And our isle ceased to be known as the Pearl of the Antilles.

Haiti's presence on the western part of the island represents an amputation of the Dominican future. What loomed ahead as the future in the middle of the sixteenth century is, in the second half of the twentieth century, a past of more than three hundred years. Thus, Dominicans cannot ignore that past in writing their history, since in the last three centuries the whole course of the lives of our people has been shaped by this factor: the existence of Haiti at our side, on a relatively small island.

The existence of the Dominican people is the result of the Spanish expansion to the west. Haiti is a result of the wars of France, England, and Holland against the Spanish empire. Over the centuries, Dominicans became a people maimed by European rivalries. Our maiming refers to nothing so concrete as having lost a land once our own to a foreign country. It is something subtler and more profound, which, consciously or otherwise, affects every phase of our lives. We Dominicans know that because Haiti is there, on the same island, we can never realize our full potential. We know that inevitably, because of the Haitian revolution, we will sooner or later be dragged down to our neighbor's level. Toward the end of the eighteenth century and the beginning of the nineteenth, nobody would invest even 1 peso in developing, for example, the Dominican sugar industry because of fear of invasions from Haiti. Haitian coffee and sugar had stopped flowing to the European and U.S. markets. Although no country was better suited to take over this production than Santo Domingo, foreign capital preferred to go to Cuba. That was the beginning of Cuba's development. The development of the Dominican Republic at first was checked and later declined, as the ablest and wealthiest people, alarmed by the Haitian revolution, left the Spanish part of the island.

Off the northwestern coast of Hispaniola is the small island of Tortuga, which the colonial Spanish Government had abandoned. It had proved too costly to supply the little island with the men and money necessary to ward off repeated English and French attacks. Tortuga passed into the hands of French pirates, and later to the French Government. Little by little, white Frenchmen left the island and gradually settled in the small fertile valleys along the northwestern edge of Hispaniola. They took slaves and began developing sugar and indigo plantations. By the time Spain realized what had been happening, a French enclave was already entrenched within its colony. These people regarded themselves, by right of conquest, as French colonists, part of the French empire, owing no allegiance to the Spanish crown. They called their part of the island Saint-Domingue. Later the name was changed to Haiti. At first, Spain, out of laziness, let them go their way. Later Spain had to recognize their existence, and finally, in the eighteenth century, weakened by continued wars in Europe, was forced to recognize Haiti's status as a colony of a foreign power.

In *Trujillo: Reasons for an Unparalleled Tyranny,* I detailed certain events in the colony of Haiti when the slaves rebelled against their masters as a consequence of the agitation unleashed by the French Revolution. It is unnecessary to repeat those details here, but I shall briefly explain that this rebellion, at the beginning of the nineteenth century, produced the Republic of Haiti. This country had been in existence for eighteen years when the Dominicans declared themselves to be independent of Spain and under the protection of Colombia. Less than two months later, Haiti sent its armies across the border and extended its government over the entire island. Thus, the Dominican Republic, established in 1844, was created out of a war against Haiti, not against the mother country of Spain.

That war, known in Dominican history as the War of Independence (although in those days it was more properly referred to as the War of Separation), was the culmination of a long struggle that had begun in the seventeenth century and lasted throughout practically the entire eighteenth century. It also produced dark pages at the beginning of the nineteenth century, with the invasions of Toussaint, Dessalines, and Christophe from Haiti. Dominicans, then, were born of fighting, first against the French in the west and later against their Haitian heirs.

I feel it necessary to repeat what I said about the Haitian revolution in my book on Trujillo: It is the only revolution in modern history that was simultaneously a war of independence (colony against metropolis), a social war (slaves against masters), and a racial war (whites against blacks). The three wars in one produced devastating violence. The former slaves destroyed in absolute, not relative, terms *every bit* of the considerable wealth that had accumulated during Haiti's colonial period. To a certain degree, this destructive aspect of the Haitian revolution seems to have been an enduring feature. Through all the years of its independence, Haiti has constantly warred against any human or social entity that could in any way become a substitute for the French colonists.

This perpetual social struggle—which had its origin in black against white, because the blacks were slaves and the whites masters—later was directed against the mulattoes, and it has been maintained as a struggle without quarter of Negroes against mulattoes. As it happened, it was the mulattoes, perhaps because they were the sons of white men and thus had more means available to them, who studied to be civil servants, businessmen, and professionals. They became the elite. Originally, they had no economic base, but later they acquired wealth and threatened to become castes with economic power. At about the time that these massacres, with their natural concomitant of political instability, were holding back the country's development, government officials used their powers to set up businesses and make themselves rich, and then took their money to Europe or, later, to the United States. This went beyond exploitation of a poor people; it was out-and-out robbery of the most miserable wretches. This went on decade after decade, while the Haitian population was growing, land was eroding, and government facilities were becoming increasingly inadequate for public health and education requirements. It was as natural as a ball rolling down a slope for Haiti to fall under François Duvalier's dictatorship. He had been ruling for many years before my democratic administration took office in the Dominican Republic.

Psychologically, Duvalier is a type of man found in primitive societies. The more power he acquires, the more he is filled with a haughtiness that day by day transforms him physically, numbing him, so that he resembles nothing so much as a puppet that keeps swelling and swelling until it must either flop over on its back or explode. His eyelids droop, his gaze becomes cold, and his face takes on a sheen as if a spell has been cast over him. His face gradually becomes frozen and his voice takes on an increasingly commanding tone that becomes lower and lower and more and more terrifying. In such creatures, the effects of power are more than physical; there are also corresponding changes in the soul, which gradually desensitize them to all human feeling, until they become only receptacles of uncontrolled passions. These men are dangerous. They create an aura of sorcery. They deny being simple human beings, mortal and fallible, and consider themselves living representatives of the dark forces that govern the world.

Anyone who doubts my description or analysis has only to glance at a photograph of Duvalier taken in, say, 1955, and then another made in 1965. They will show two different men, the Haitian version of Oscar Wilde's Dorian Gray.

On the south side of the border dividing Haiti from the Dominican Republic, one can, from time to time, see men of Duvalier's stamp, who were ordinary peasants until they felt themselves possessed with a power they call religious and began giving prescriptions, recommending cures, making up their own rites. They then took on the appearance of forest *caudillos*. They are mad with power, as Hitler was on a much grander scale.

As soon as I was elected President of the Dominican Republic, Duvalier resolved to kill me—why, I have no idea. Perhaps he had a dream about me and interpreted it as an order to do away with me. Perhaps in a voodoo trance, one of his guardian spirits told him that I would become his enemy. He chose as my murderer one of Trujillo's old spies, a man who had been the Haitian Consul in Camaguey, Cuba. During the political campaign, I never mentioned Duvalier. The UCN made various declarations about his tyranny, and if I remember correctly, Fiallo referred to him. I avoided mention of foreign problems. It did not seem prudent to introduce them, and besides, if I was elected, it would be unwise to enter the presidency committed to foreign-policy statements made during the heat of the campaign. I, therefore, had not done anything to arouse Duvalier's enmity. It was unearned, and I must assume that it had supernatural origins.

After reading about the attitude of the Dominican people toward the existence of Haiti, and the long history of hostility between the two countries, it should not be difficult to imagine Dominican reaction to the radio bulletin that Duvalier's police had stormed our Embassy in Port-au-Prince, Haiti's capital. Within an hour our people were aroused, political parties were holding emergency meetings, and telegrams denouncing the aggression were flooding the National Palace.

A few weeks before, in Haiti, acts of terrorism were directed against the Duvalier government, which thereupon requested the withdrawal of the U.S. military mission. High-ranking military officials were arrested and jailed. A certain Barbot, the man who had founded Duvalier's armed militia (known as the *tonton macoutes,* black killers), was making assaults on the outskirts of Port-au-Prince.

Persecuted civilians and military took refuge in the various Latin American diplomatic missions; several were hiding in the Dominican Embassy. One day a Haitian lieutenant named Benoît came to our Embassy and asked for asylum. It was granted, of course. The following day, Barbot's men fired on Duvalier's automobile, which was taking the dictator's children to school. Duvalier's response was immediate. His killers entered the house of Benoît's family, killed everyone in it, including Benoît's mother and a little girl, and burned the place to the ground. At the same time, an attack was made on the Dominican Embassy. This, of course, was tantamount to an attack on our country.

That day was a Sunday, if my memory serves me, and it was the beginning of May. Suddenly we began receiving bulletins indicating that Duvalier was planning something. Relatives of Trujillo's were entering Haiti, armed Haitian guards had surrounded our Embassy in Port-au-Prince, diplomatic pouches were being held at the border, and our Consul in the border village of Belladere had been imprisoned.

That night, on radio and television, I publicly denounced these mad acts of Duvalier's. Meanwhile, the Foreign Office was drafting cables to Port-au-Prince and to the OAS, and preparing press releases. After my address, I began to formulate a plan of action, to free Haitians and Dominicans from the dangers that might be unloosed on countries by the madness of a leader obviously out of his mind. It was a simple plan, and would cost not a single drop of blood. The Dominican Republic would mobilize its troops and mass them on the southern border at the point closest to Haiti's capital. The mobilization would be made in such a way as to give the unmistakable impression of a military advance on Haiti. Once the proper climate had thus been prepared, the Dominican Air Force would fly over Port-au-Prince and bombard the city with quantities of leaflets in French, asking the people of the Haitian capital to evacuate the area of the Presidential Palace because Dominican planes would be bombing it in a matter of hours. I was sure that because of the consequent state of agitation in Haiti and the impression of military preparation in the Dominican Republic, Duvalier would flee before a single bullet need be fired.

But the plan had one flaw. I could confide it to no one, not even the military commanders who would participate in it. If I told anyone that all these movements were to be phony, that we were not to go to war, my plan would soon be known. And I had to expect irresponsibility from most of the leaders of the so-called opposition. One of them, maybe even two or three, would in all certainty appear before a microphone to make a mockery of my scheme. In fact, right in the middle of the crisis, one of those leaders accused me of inventing the whole episode in order to win myself a place in history as the conqueror of Haiti. How absurd! If the Dominicans conquered Haiti, all that they would accomplish would be to buy at a high price the problems of Haiti, to be added to Dominican problems.

When something is not completely finished, Dominican peasants say that "the tail is yet to be skinned," referring to the tail of a freshly slaughtered pig. In the case of my plan, there was a tail yet to be skinned. What would happen if the Haitian dictator failed to play his assigned role and did not run? There was only one answer: Dominican troops would have to advance onto Haitian territory at least a few miles, enough to give the impression of a genuine attack. I was sure that the Haitian people in the border region would offer no resistance. If absolutely necessary, the Air Force could drop two or three bombs where they would cause no casualties.

At this point a mystery arose. Dominican generals came to tell me that their trucks had no spare tires and were in no condition to transport troops. Who had told them to use that alibi? Until the previous night, all of them had enthusiastically supported the mobilization plan, and now, suddenly, the military trucks were out of commission.

Ambassador Martin came to see me. He was quite alarmed. It was the first time I had ever seen him alarmed. The possibility of a Dominican-Haitian war had greatly upset him, undoubtedly because it had upset the State Department. And at that moment, Moscow, Peking, Havana, and the MPD in Santo Domingo were all charging that if I attacked Haiti, I would be acting as a puppet of "Yankee imperialism." The situation was sadly comic. It was precisely "Yankee imperialism" that was impeding the Dominican decision to settle the Haitian problem.

Suddenly, a few days later, Martin visited me at home to tell me that his government expected Duvalier to leave Haiti within hours. At that very moment, a KLM plane was waiting at the Port-au-Prince airport to take him to New York, and from there to Amsterdam, and on to Algiers, where President Ben Bella had offered him asylum. I was doubtful. "Duvalier will not go," I said. Martin assured me that he would. In the course of the day, Martin dropped in again, and that night he phoned twice to keep me informed of what was happening in Haiti. The following morning at five o'clock he came to see me still convinced that Duvalier would leave. I again told him: "He will not go." And Duvalier did not go.

A few days later, I ran into a Cuban exile who told me that Dominican officers were training Haitians at a military base in the interior. How was such a thing possible without my knowledge? I called the Minister of the Armed Forces, questioned him, learned that the story was true, and immediately ordered the encampment to be disbanded. It was one thing to settle matters with Duvalier under favorable conditions, in the open, as a democracy should always act. It was quite another to prepare Haitian troops to launch an invasion of their country. This would be a violation of the principle of nonintervention, and could make us lose our authority if the current Caribbean turmoil led another power to play the same game. At that moment, I decided to wait for a propitious opportunity to seek a solution to the problem of Duvalier.

One fine day thereafter, I read in the papers early one morning that a Haitian General named Léon Cantave had invaded the north coast of Haiti. He had been to see me to ask for my support, and I had answered that the Dominican Government could not help him. Then where had his expedition come from? Who had armed it? Who was behind it? This was a mystery that must be cleared up. I called together my military leaders and reviewed every possibility. I asked if any of them knew what kind of arms Cantave might be using. No one knew. According to the reports, Cantave had not launched his attack from Dominican territory, he had received no help from the Dominican Armed Forces, and the Dominican arsenals contained no weapons of the type he had carried to Haiti.

Something was wrong. If Cantave had not left from Dominican territory, he would have had to set out from a neighboring island—the Bahamas, perhaps, which were under the British flag. And if this was so, who had helped him? I openly asked the same question of Ambassador Martin. He said that he had no idea, nor had his government, but that some of his aides presumed that Cantave had had help from Venezuela. This seemed impossible to me. In the first place, Betancourt had Communist guerrillas on his own soil and would not endorse an act similar to Fidel Castro's attack on the Venezuelan Government. In the second place, if Betancourt had had anything to do with Cantave's invasion, he would have informed me of it. And so I laughed and asked Martin: "Is there any place in Florida called Venezuela?" "No, no, there isn't," he answered, and laughed, too.

Several days before my government was overthrown, I was in my office in the National Palace at about six in the morning when the chief military aide told me that the Haitians were attacking Dajabón, a Dominican village on the northern border. Bullets were being fired from the Haitian side, at Villa de Juana Méndez (Ouanaminthe, in the Haitian patois), about a mile and a quarter away. As reports began coming through a few hours later, I learned the truth. Cantave had entered Haiti again and had attacked the garrison at Juana Méndez. The battle had continued for some time, with considerable rifle and machine-gun fire. Where had Cantave obtained, a second time, the arms and ammunition for an attack?

The next day, to my amazement, I saw a picture in the Dominican papers showing Cantave in the Dajabón barracks. He had crossed the border, as had other Haitians, some of them wounded. But Cantave was dressed as if he were on his way to a gala ball rather than just returning from combat. This meant that the Haitian General kept clothes in Dajabón, or somewhere else nearby. For the first time, my suspicions had located a thread that was to lead me to the spool. I called the Minister of Foreign Affairs and the Minister of the Armed Forces. I said to the former: "Please request the OAS to send in a commission to establish that the aggression against Haiti does not originate on Dominican soil."

Did this move have anything to do with the *coup d'état?*

I often think so. If, as I had hoped, the OAS had investigated and gotten to the bottom of matters, I would have discovered what hidden hand was pulling the strings and causing my administration to appear ridiculous, which reflected, of course, on its President, who, in the eyes of his country and the international agencies, was responsible for

Dominican foreign policy. The same manipulation had also exposed us to the madness of a dictator capable of anything.

I hope that someday a solution will be found to the mystery of all the strange Dominican-Haitian incidents that occurred in 1963.

The Role of Corruption
in the Coup

In Latin American countries, with very few exceptions, both the ruled and the rulers practice corruption in the most natural ways. Corruption is by no means confined to stealing public funds, but extends to other situations in society. When the democratic regime came to power in the Dominican Republic, it had to make an effort to reawaken morality in the country or risk the destruction of democracy by immorality.

A week after taking over their official duties, the Ministers of the Treasury and Public Works knew, more or less, how thievery was organized in their departments. Under an agreement they made with the Minister of the Armed Forces, he chose from the military school a few students who possessed certain qualities. With the help of this group, the two Ministers organized the first important campaign against stealing the public's money.

Several thousand men were employed by the government to clean the gutters that lined the highways. The expense amounted to 1,250,000 pesos a month, or 15 million pesos a year. Because these men were working on a project labeled "emergency," their wages were not included in the federal budget and had to be rounded up from any other sources available. (This statistic offers some idea of how federal spending was set up and how it operated. The 1963 budget had been approved three months before by the Council of State.) The emergency plan was supposed to pay semi-monthly salaries. When the democratic government came to power, payments were forty-five days behind schedule. In addition, two months' pay was still owed the workers for the previous year. Each laborer carried a card indicating the number of days' pay due him. The country was divided into several public-works zones. Money was sent from the capital to pay the wages, and workers presented their cards for redemption at the headquarters in each zone.

If the prescribed system was followed, there was no margin for thievery. Each worker had a card as proof of the amount owed him. He would hardly allow himself to be cheated. Yet someone ingeniously devised a way to get money out of the central fund. The method was simple— paying wages late. If payday was held off for a week, or ten days, or even two weeks, workers would become hungry enough to sell their pay cards at a discount or exchange them for food at stores in their area. And so a single businessman, or two at most, could get control of operations in the paymaster's headquarters of each zone. The businessman received additional cards and divided the money with the person who gave them to him.

Under the new PRD administration, the first wage payment to these workers was made by the unknown group of youths who for one or two days had exchanged their military uniforms for civilian clothes. They required that each card, to be redeemed, must be presented by the worker.

When the workers explained that that was impossible, that they had cashed in their cards at stores, it was simple enough to present the storekeepers with the workers' names and obtain proof that fraud had taken place. When the youths came back to the capital, they brought with them a surplus over the payroll of more than 150,000 pesos. From that single government expenditure, corruption had been taking 4 million pesos a year, more than 2 per cent of the nation's total budget.

The anti-theft campaign, aimed at every area of potential fraud, was so effected that after the administration's first month, we estimated that by the end of that fiscal year, nine months later, we would have saved 10 million pesos. This in no way indicates that the end of the abuse was in sight. According to our calculations, thievery in fiscal matters alone exceeded 25 million pesos a year and might approach 30 million—almost 20 per cent of the total budget. We could not even guess at the illegal sums taken from autonomous agencies, and from farms, properties, and other state enterprises. Neither could we estimate the money lost to the government through contraband, cheating on taxes, and capricious tax exemptions.

It was impossible to do everything at once. We appointed as Minister of Public Properties a businessman with importing experience, who in seven months recovered automobiles, furniture, real estate, and cattle for the state, readjusted rents on government-owned houses, and collected back taxes. To the Development Corporation, which administered most government enterprises, went a like-minded director, who placed a new manager at the head of every company within his jurisdiction. When the government fell on September 25, 1963, the only areas in which reorganization was still pending were the state sugar industry and the elimination of fraud in government purchasing.

The latter was the most widespread. When Trujillo came to power in 1930, the country had had a centralized State Purchasing Department, which had purchased supplies through public bidding. When the dictator died, each Ministry and department had control over its own purchasing. Dominican businessmen and their agents abroad had become accustomed to handing over to the government agent 10- or 15-per cent commissions on a government purchase order. Thus the democratic administration found itself saddled with a practice that had reached scandalous proportions. Frequently a department officer made unnecessary purchases simply to collect the commission. Or he allowed prices to be raised in order to collect a higher commission. Or he managed to ruin new equipment in order to justify a requisition and, consequently, a commission.

It is difficult to imagine how much these commission frauds amounted to. They encompassed every manner and variety of activity. Public-works contractors had to pay a commission to an intermediary, who in turn paid a commission to his boss. Subcontractors paid a commission to contractors. The chain reached down through the lowest public official, who had to pay a kickback in order to hold his job. Even the clerk who made out government checks collected a commission from the people to whom they were made out.

Part of the Dominican middle class thrived on this widespread corruption—those who had not prepared themselves to obtain benefits on the basis of ability in honest and open competition. Shady deals, out-and-out fraud, and government favors were common practice. Therein lay the key to the middle class, not only in the Dominican Republic, but throughout the rest of Latin America at one time or another. This was the explanation of the middle class's failure to support the new democratic regime, since under the new government, there was constant risk of public denunciation, through rallies, the radio, and the press, of all these corrupt practices. While a blanket charge of corruption is used by unscrupulous politicians to attack everybody, legitimate denunciations scare those who live off fraud and lead them to desire the elimination of the government that permits the public denunciations.

Corruption produces undesirable results in another area. It disillusions those who have placed their faith in democracy, especially the young people. This is particularly true in Latin America, where perhaps because of this tradition of dishonesty or because of the necessity to compensate for it in order to establish the balance that life demands, young people have an urgent need for public morality to govern the actions of those in power.

I knew, through private sources, that in the Army, Air Force, Navy, and police, commission-collecting was a habit. I also knew that the service chiefs were accustomed to naming procurement officials to split commissions with them, and that as soon as one of these officials had accumulated sufficient money, a replacement was named to split the take. This institutionalized thievery reached such a point that at dawn on September 25, even before the coup proclamation was signed, the military was discussing the matter of commissions and arranging for the appointment of new procurement men every six months. It was even decided in what order the signers of the proclamation would be named to these spots. The authority to collect commissions was the price paid for the murder of a democracy.

One day I called together the leaders of the services and told them that there would be no more commission-taking. I explained that Dominican democracy was in the limelight all over Latin America and that we could not permit it to be dishonored. Dishonesty dishonors a democracy not only because fraud is a crime, but also because public funds that should be destined for works and services of public benefit are used to line private pockets. I went on to explain that, according to my information, most of this money taken from the people was converted into dollars and sent abroad, where it was placed in personal accounts, and that while on paper it appeared to be deposited in the name of a private citizen, it was actually going to foreign businessmen, corporations, and industries, since the banks used the money they received as deposits to finance business. Thus Dominican money that left the Dominican Republic was being used to finance countries other than our own. The Dominican Republic was potentially a rich country, I told them, and if for two years, just a bare two years, we could hold to an austerity program, and make honesty a habit in the administration of public funds, the resulting development of the country would make it possible to have wealth for all.

I was aware that among these service chiefs there was one who was not benefiting from organized thievery, but that the procurement officials in his department were doing what their counterparts were doing in every branch of the Armed Forces. Of the group before me, it was the police chief who listened most attentively to what I was saying. The following day he asked to see me. "Mr. President," he said, "my orders have gone out to drop the commissions to 5 per cent. Cutting them out overnight is almost impossible. Next month I shall order them not to collect any more. But," he went on, "I want to ask you something. What do we do if the businessmen we deal with insist on paying the commission?"

"Tell them to lower their prices instead," I said. "These men don't give commissions out of their profits. What they do is raise the price." I mention these details to make it clear how routinely the agent charged with uncovering the thievery accepted the practice of taking commissions.

A week later I called the service leaders together again to learn how they were carrying out my instructions. According to them, kickbacks had been eliminated from the Armed Forces. I opened a drawer of my desk and took out a receipt that an official had given a state-owned factory that manufactured batteries. The receipt clearly stated the amount of the commission—15 per cent—and the intended use of the merchandise—as batteries for Air Force trucks and cars. The Minister of the Armed Forces took the receipt with him and never again permitted a single division of his Ministry, or even of the police, to buy a battery from that factory. Henceforth purchases were made from merchants who paid commissions in cash and left no telltale evidence of the transaction.

Corruption took many forms. Nepotism was one of them, for under Trujillo, the country had acquired the custom of installing entire families in departments where one of them had become chief. The expense of this was outrageous. When my administration came to power, we found a storeroom of whisky, wine, and other liquor in the National Palace. Automobiles with official license plates appeared everywhere. While I was President, I used neither a state automobile nor official license plates. I wanted to set an example of simplicity and austerity. In the National Palace, toasts were drunk only in coffee or coconut milk. The Dominican Republic was a poor country and would have to bear its poverty with dignity, without shame, and without drawing attention to it by flaunting luxuries that were too limited in supply to go very far. When my wife made a trip to the United States to take care of our son, who had had an operation, I ordered customs inspectors at the airport to open her luggage and subject any new purchases to the same import duties that any ordinary citizen would pay. My Cabinet members and all high-ranking officials behaved just as I did.

In order to eliminate the sale of import permits and the consequent high prices of imported goods, all controls were taken off and free import was established. Lottery agents were ruled out by law, to wipe out their practice of buying tickets from the state and reselling them at a profit to ticket vendors. Studies were made on mechanizing state accounting, with the goal of preventing fraud in tax calculations. At the time of the coup, a purchasing commission was being set up to put an end to the kickback system.

Just by eliminating stealing from funds on hand and the escape of tax money before it came to the Treasury, the country could have paid its bills without having to increase taxes. It could have set aside a good share of this money for productive investments and to build up the infrastructure. The latter was a matter of life or death for the nation. In the Dominican Republic, the investment in infrastructure was less than a fifth of what it should be. Puerto Rico, with a million inhabitants fewer and a sixth as much territory, had invested no less than $2 billion in roads, aqueducts, schools, hospitals, seaports, airports, electric plants, bridges, and other works. The Dominican investment in such projects was less than $500 million.

For years and years, open and well-organized corruption had run rampant, from the top of the ladder down. It would not be easy to do away with it. But at least it was already known that the top level of public power was no longer backing corruption—and, in fact, was actively opposing it. Little by little, the habit of respecting the people's property could be created. But the task was a difficult one. The beneficiaries of immorality were defending their right to practice it with more ardor than they would have used to defend a legitimate right. For these people, it was the government that was committing a crime, the unpardonable crime of exercising honesty and demanding it from every citizen.

While the government advanced its objectives, the opposition countered with righteous wrath. A radio "commentator"—more properly a scandalmonger, whose stock-in-trade was principally insults, lies, and vulgarity—who had been managing editor of the government newspaper under the Council of State, was indicted for improper use of the newspaper's funds. When he was about to be arrested, opposition leaders—including the former UCN presidential candidate, Fiallo, and the former candidate of one of the marginal parties—rallied round him in a television studio before the cameras, so that the TV audience could witness the sad spectacle, and shouted that freedom of expression was being destroyed and that they were going to give their lives to save it. A few loudly demanded that the military overthrow the government. One even beseeched Trujillo's assassins to come forth and repeat the heroic deed of May 30, 1961.

The intensity of the corruption can be measured by such an episode. The top opposition leaders resisted justice being done in a case of common ordinary abuse of confidence represented by the dishonest handling of public funds. It was truly depressing. In few countries could two former presidential candidates meet to participate in such a spectacle. As was inevitable, these two former presidential candidates signed the proclamation that established the coup government. In a memorable photograph taken on September 25, the two appear with the officials who only a few hours before had reached an agreement with the military on the sequence of administrators.

I have said "as was inevitable" because the conspiracy to overthrow the government was a natural outgrowth of the corruption from which a sector of the middle class acquired its illegal gains. The overthrow of the democratic government, which had been voted in by an overwhelming majority in elections adjudged impeccable by the entire world, was simply another way of cheating the people, since it stole from them what they had created, and it stole from them their hope. The coup was, furthermore, an armed attack, carried out in the dark of night, treacherously and furtively. It was an assault, plain and simple, and those who induced it and carried it out were guilty of a crime far more serious than that of the miserable "commentator" who had misused a few pesos. But both crimes were born of the same disease—corruption. In both cases, the end was the same: to take something that belonged to somebody else. In both cases, that something belonged to the Dominican people.

A few days after the military coup that put Batista in power in Cuba in 1952, a Jamaican Negro who was driving a taxi in Havana said something that impressed me. "Batista had to do this, because he's a man who doesn't know how to lose," he observed. "No one can be a good citizen without knowing how to lose." I remember thinking at the time that a man who cannot lose cannot win, either. He tries to win by grabbing whatever others have. In underdeveloped countries, sports are taught solely to produce strong muscles. Unfortunately, young athletes are taught nothing about sportsmanship and the character-building aspects of sports, which are of far greater consequence than bulging biceps to show off on the beach or in photo contests. The principal aim of competitive games is to develop a team spirit, a temperate character, and the sportsmanship that enables a winner to triumph without arrogance and a loser to accept defeat without humiliation.

Corruption takes a thousand forms in Latin American countries, and the result is that corruption corrupts. Because of the failure to punish the men guilty of these illegal practices and because of their display of the things bought with the profits of their stealing, corruption spreads to different levels. Thievery is at the root of every Latin American dictatorship—stealing committed that has to be defended, stealing yet to be committed, continuance of illegal privileges by certain social groups, and an eagerness to rob on the part of whoever wants to be dictator. And hard on the heels of thievery come other crimes, as the thieves try to protect themselves. To do so, they must suppress the people's liberty, and to accomplish this necessitates terrorism, and terrorism enters by means of murder.

Although there were many other factors, the Dominican coup of 1963 was principally caused by corruption. On my trip to Mexico, as the guest of President López Mateos, to celebrate the anniversary of Mexican independence, I took along with me the Minister of the Armed Forces and the head of the Air Force. During the trip, the latter presented to me a plan of his to purchase $6 million worth of English war planes. I had already seen some reports on the proposed transaction. The man had held several meetings in the Hotel Embajador in Santo Domingo with foreign representatives, at which they had discussed arrangements for the purchase over drinks. Only someone totally irresponsible would think that a country on the verge of bankruptcy, with its people dying of hunger, could afford to spend $6 million on war planes. The general was fully aware, as were his fellow officers, of the government's financial situation, since I frequently spoke to him about it. Yet his mentality had been such that he had gone ahead, without discussing it with me, and assembled a group of pilots to bring those planes from Britain. He had already enrolled them in an English class.

The customary commission for Armed Forces purchases was 10 per cent, although in some cases—for example, the one involving those batteries—it reached 15 per cent. During those conferences at the Hotel Embajador the fee had been set at 20 per cent; that came to $1.2 million. This was a really enormous sum, and it was worth it to overthrow a government whose President was so averse to allowing $1.2 million of the Dominican people's money to end up in a bank account in Miami or Puerto Rico.

I returned home from Mexico on September 19. The coup was decided on four days later. At dawn on the twenty-fifth, the event took place.

Trujillo—Military Chief
of the Coup

The Dominican Armed Forces provided a perfect cross section of the country's sociological make-up, but certain
qualities were more evident in the Armed Forces than in
Dominican society. The military institutes in Santo Domingo were made up of men interested in neither military
service nor a military career, with few exceptions; these
men were earning their living, receiving a salary, and always aiming at the capture of a certain position, a situation
not unlike that existing under Batista in Cuba.

Military service was not required for Dominican men.
Contracts were offered for a fixed period and a fixed wage.
A soldier naturally tried to advance as rapidly as possible.
His promotions were usually rewards for his adaptability
to the methods and whims of Trujillo, his son Ramfis, or
any one of the innumerable chiefs who belonged to the
Trujillo family. Success came quickest to the man with the
most ambition and the fewest scruples. The Army offered

rapid social mobility. A common soldier with the right combination of qualities could rise very quickly through the ranks to major, colonel, and finally general, and thereby leave the peasant class for the middle and upper strata of the middle class. The rapid ascent from one class to another transformed the man. He became increasingly conservative, less tolerant, harder, more concerned about his own well-being and less sensitive to the country's ills. All these characteristics were common to Dominican society as a whole, but they stood out with greater clarity in the Armed Forces.

The Dominican Armed Forces had been organized in 1916 by the United States military occupation government which had dissolved the previous Army. At the beginning, the new Army functioned as a rural police, and was called the Dominican National Police, although the people referred to the men as "the Guards." Men were recruited chiefly from unemployed peasants and former soldiers, who contracted for a two-year term, with the right to renew the contract as many times as they wished. A few members of the lower stratum of the middle class, among them Trujillo, joined this force as officers. After Trujillo came to power, it was easy to jump from private to officer in a single day, simply by a demonstration of fervent Trujilloism—for example, by killing one of the Chief's enemies. Even during his last days, Trujillo would suddenly ask an officer, "How many have you killed?" He would do this to the officers he invited to eat with him. I know of one officer who managed to avoid these dinners because, he told me, "If he had asked me that question, I have no idea what I would have done. Probably something crazy."

That officer, who got angry every time he recalled his narrow escape, was one of the eighty or a hundred officers who had entered the Armed Forces to begin a professional career based on ability and worth, without realizing what it was like inside the organization under Trujillo. Such officers had great difficulty in getting responsible posts. The social structure in the Armed Forces hierarchy did not let them past the level of the lower middle class.

How can lower, middle, and upper strata of the middle class exist in an army?

As I have said, this was an army that offered a means of earning a living, of acquiring economic and social standing. In terms of Army ranks, the masses were represented by the buck privates and trainees. The lower stratum of the middle class took in the ranks of second lieutenant and extended up as far as captain and sometimes major. The middle stratum included Air Force majors, who received extra wages, and lieutenant colonels and colonels. The upper stratum was comprised of active and retired generals. Retired generals received the same salary as active generals, but enjoyed less income, since they did not participate in many business enterprises involving government money, as active generals did.

During Trujillo's first twenty-five years in power, maintainance of public order was entrusted to the police, and political control to the Armed Forces. Later, political repression was concentrated within the Military Intelligence Services (Servicios de Inteligencia Militar, or SIM). Every department had its SIM agent, and wherever SIM was, crime and horrible torture followed. But in 1959, as a result of the anti-Trujillo invasion launched from Cuba, SIM lost its exclusive jurisdiction, and control was again exercised by officers and soldiers in all the forces, especially the Air Force, which was commanded by the dictator's son, Ramfis, until late in 1961.

The Air Force's most powerful installation was the San Isidro Air Base, some nine miles from the capital. The military school, a recent creation, was located in the same vicinity. One day, while I was doing some work at my house and the heads of the Armed Forces were waiting for me on a small patio adjoining my room, I heard the Air Force commander talking to his fellow generals. It seemed that the younger officers were worried by the use that was being made of freedom of speech. Everyone was talking on the radio, the commander said, and under the constitutional government, everyone wanted to show that he was brave by saying whatever he pleased. Many young officers were frankly afraid. A number of them had had to carry out a few rather ruthless orders. "Remember," said the Air Force commander, "that the cadets had to kill those boys of the 14th of June."

When I came onto the terrace, I gave no indication that I had overheard their conversation. A few days later I questioned a young officer whom I trusted. The "boys of the 14th of June" had been the invaders from Cuba who had landed on Dominican soil on June 14, 1959, the date from which came the name of the 14th of June Movement. Most of these invaders had been taken prisoner. They had been brutally beaten, kicked, and wounded, and then taken to the San Isidro base. There they had been tortured mercilessly, and finally, without a trial, they had been shot to death in the courtyard of the military school. The director of the military school had personally selected the cadets for the firing squad. If any cadet had refused to participate in the slaughter, the director would have lined him up with the other victims. Of course, the director of the military school had to be, and was, one of the most active organizers of my administration's overthrow. In fact, on the morning of the coup, he went from group to group saying that he had pretended to be my friend in order to be able to topple me without arousing my suspicions. This gives an idea of the morality common to the coup's military chiefs. A man who wears a uniform is less entitled than anyone else to deceive. In every instance, however, the deceiver is a low creature.

To give an idea of the character of the Dominican Army of Trujillo—which was the same army I inherited when I took office—I shall relate a truly tragic incident. But first I should explain that my gratitude to those who assassinated Trujillo, and thereby released my country from a tyranny of fear and the Americas from a shameful blemish, is almost like that of a son to his mother, and if it is not the same, this is because between son and mother there exists, besides gratitude, a perpetual bond of love. Without the mother, there would be no son. And without Trujillo's death, I should never have been permitted to become, if only for a short time, a Dominican with the right and the ability to live in my land, to return to the bosom of my lost country, to feel myself again a part of my native surroundings. As I feel a gratitude toward those who killed Trujillo, I also feel admiration, in different degrees, for each of them. The one I admire most is Lieutenant Amado García Guerrero, a soldier of the people and an extraordinary man by anyone's standards.

García Guerrero survived Trujillo's death by only two or three days. He was hunted down and shot by Ramfis' assassins. He was fortunate enough to die fighting; his accomplices were not. As he is no longer living, he cannot confirm what I am going to relate. But I am sure every word is true, because it was told me by someone who had heard it from García's own lips.

Lieutenant García Guerrero, a man of humble origin, had that integrity and moral fiber that are found in the common people of the Dominican Republic but not in the middle class, except under rare circumstances. Because he was serious and decisive, he had been taken into Trujillo's corps of aides. Once there, hearing his companions talking about details of the dictator's life and seeing the man for

himself, he developed a rabid hatred for Trujillo. Sickened
to the depths of his soul by the coarseness, the baseness, the
vanity, the greed, and the utter evil of that man, he resolved to rid his country of the ruffian who had reduced
the Republic to a preserve for crime. He entered into a
plot that was to culminate in the tyrant's death on May
30, 1961. Because of his post in Trujillo's military family,
he became a key figure in the conspiracy. It would have
been very difficult, perhaps impossible, to succeed in the
assassination without García Guerrero, since he was the
one who knew the dictator's movements and passed this
information on to the plotters.

García Guerrero had been involved in the plot for more
than a month when, one midnight, he received a call
ordering him to appear at SIM headquarters. When he
walked into the house of torture, "the Forty," as it was
called, he saw an assemblage of bloody human wrecks too
weak even to groan. "I have called you to kill that man,"
the SIM chief told him, indicating a figure seated in a
chair. García Guerrero thought quickly: "They know
something and are testing me. If I refuse to do what is
asked of me, they will torture me to get the names of my
companions; if I do not refuse, they will believe in me and
in what I tell them."

The valor required of García Guerrero, being the up-
right man he was, not to respond by striking or shooting
the killer who ordered him to take a man's life, involves
something beyond ordinary bravery. He must remain calm,
display no hesitancy, so as to spare himself and his companions for the act that would free the country of a dictator and his regime. He took the pistol held out to him
by the SIM chief and killed the unknown man.

Who was the victim? A Dominican, but a Dominican
who died to free his people. Perhaps he had been taken to
SIM headquarters because he was suspected of the same

sort of planning that García Guerrero was involved in. The intensity of García Guerrero's anguish in that moment and the days that followed was immeasurable. He had resolved, with deep passion, cold reason, and strong will, to eliminate a man who steeped the country in crime, and in order to achieve this, he had had to become a part of that monstrous machinery that was Trujilloism. From that night on, Lieutenant García Guerrero lived only to assassinate Trujillo. He had the satisfaction of seeing his mission accomplished and Trujillo's body, transformed in a single instant from absolute ruler of a nation to lifeless chunk of flesh, dumped in the trunk of a car.

García Guerrero was only one of many officers taken to SIM headquarters and commanded to kill. "How many have you killed?" Trujillo would ask, in his high-pitched voice and offensive accents. Some men killed because a refusal to do so would jeopardize their own lives. Others killed because they had the souls of killers. Still others killed because it was a sure way to distinguish themselves and gain promotions and favors. But there were some officers, as I have said, who had joined the Armed Forces to enter on a professional career, who had believed that in a military career they could serve their country. These were men who wanted to study, to prepare themselves, to qualify for advancement. Most of them were from the lower stratum of the middle class, and some were from the middle stratum. It was very difficult for these officers to get top posts. The high command feared them and closed all the roads to promotion. It feared their honesty and their military education, and it always arranged for them to be out of the country or in posts where they vegetated like bureaucrats.

During the year between the flight of Trujillo's family in November, 1961, and the elections of December, 1962, the Armed Forces began to settle into the same pattern as the civilians. As the upper stratum of the middle class had taken power through the Council of State in order to endow itself with economic substance, so did the upper stratum of the middle class in the military assume control of the military institutes with a view to making as much money as possible as quickly as possible and then getting all the dollars it could out of the country. There may have been one or two exceptions, but no more. The Council of State established military canteens through which high-ranking military officials became businessmen. At the same time, the businessmen were meddling with the politicians in order to make politics with the military.

After the 1963 coup, Dominican big business grew alarmed at the competition from the military canteens and the contraband flooding in by sea and air via military ships and planes. The Dominican upper middle class, who through their political leaders persuaded the military to undertake the coup, thought that the military were going to be their servants. They had forgotten the lesson that Trujillo had taught. In a country like the Dominican Republic, still in the process of sorting itself out culturally, socially, and economically, the Army is nobody's instrument. When the military go out of their barracks, they go out to command, not to obey.

In a society so structurally weak that it totters on the verge of collapse, it seems logical that the Army should be similarly weak. Nevertheless, when one says "Dominican Armed Forces," the military of another country are apt to think of a stable institution, carrying out orders in a manner worthy of a soldier, but this would be an error. Consider this example of Dominican military practice. To get rid of an officer deemed unworthy of the confidence of his fellow officers—usually because he felt that the military should not intervene in politics or business—the chief of the Air Force would have a soldier steal the officer's pistol, then accuse the officer of losing or selling it, an accusation punishable by immediate discharge and loss of pension rights. These were Trujillo's tactics, to the letter.

The behavior of the Air Force chief and of many other military chiefs had all of Trujillo's hallmarks: mistresses here and there, interminable drinking sessions, filthy language, comic books, unspeakable manners, profound resentment, an existence without a single noble aim, insatiable greed for money and pleasures, total absence of loyalty to friends, family, country, or anything else. These men had risen in a few years from the poor lower stratum of the middle class—or even from the peasant class and the unemployed—to the upper stratum. In their rapid ascent up the social ladder, they had acquired all the vices of the middle and upper strata and none of the virtues. And the virtues of the Dominican middle and upper strata are not numerous.

Such people might be able to support a debauched democracy in a wealthy country, particularly a democracy that had twenty-five or thirty years ahead of it in which to continue gradually developing, progressively strengthening its social structure. But the Dominican Republic was not a rich country but a very poor country, plagued by pressing needs, unable to waste a single peso on something not absolutely essential. Furthermore, it did not have plenty of time for gradual progress, because its evolution had been held back too long. By 1961, it had reached the point where its problems were multiplying faster than their solutions. Finally, it was a country that required a model of a democracy before its eyes, a democracy as perfect as any dreamed of during that long, thirty-year night. Without such an example, the country would never believe in democracy.

It was impossible to change the Army in seven months, or even in several years. A third of a century of bad habits is not dismissed with a stroke of the pen. The Armed Forces were Trujillo's, molded by him, although born of the United States occupation; those generals and colonels were his creatures. They had been his instruments to terrorize the people. As soon as the legal and constitutional framework was withdrawn, the military would revert to what it had been until November 18, 1961—the day the Trujillos left the country—one year and ten months before the coup of 1963.

It is incredible how men can be blinded by passions and how they can be driven mad by the inability to learn to lose. I do not speak of ordinary people. These were cultivated men, political leaders—although some of those in Santo Domingo read and wrote with difficulty; they were former presidential candidates, doctors and teachers, lawyers and priests, businessmen and industrialists. Incredibly, all these people who participated in the conspiracy leading to the 1963 coup knew that the high command of the Dominican Armed Forces was still under the influence of Trujillo and that as soon as respect for the Constitution was destroyed, as soon as law and legitimate authority were toppled, the military leaders would go back to doing what they had always done: killing and plundering throughout the country.

Behavior is not accidental. And the fact that an antisocial man behaves like a normal member of society for a year does not mean that he has ceased to be antisocial at the core. In Trujillo's Armed Forces were men who had been forced to kill and plunder, and only God and their own hearts knew how much suffering this had cost them. They were never, in their innermost conscience, guilty of any crime. But there were other men who reveled in killing and plundering. When society's restraints broke down, they resumed their criminal behavior. And the conspirators behind the *coup d'état*—the political leaders, the priests, the businessmen, and the newspapermen who planned the coup and pulled the military out of the barracks to do their dirty work for them—must have known this. On their shoulders falls the burden of guilt for the murders and robberies unleashed in the Dominican Republic by the coup of September 25, 1963.

The coup was a failure in achieving its economic and political aims. Six months later, of all the parties participating in the coup, only the UCN held government posts. If the economic situation in the country had been gloomy before, it was black now. The leaders of the coup began saying, at first cautiously and then openly, that they had had no part in the plot. Military leaders with little or no awareness of history were satisfied to accept the "honor" of responsibility for the overthrow. The politicians behind the coup had become so cynical that on July 25, 1964, the UCN released a press communiqué formally opposing any sort of *coup d'état*. The military had notices published in newspapers as far away as Miami affirming their "apolitical" stand and their respect for "legitimate authority."

Perhaps I have unfairly used the word cynical. Following the overthrow, Fiallo explained more than once that "politics is opportunity." For many people, this is true. But there are a variety of opportunities to be seized and the concepts surrounding them and the words expressing them also vary. Perhaps, then, it was not cynical to condemn the staging of a coup ten months after doing precisely that and then signing a document purporting to consecrate it as a legitimate political act.

In Santo Domingo's National Palace—a creation of Trujillo's that tried to reproduce in Portland cement the noble stone and brick structures of the Italian Renaissance—there are two offices on the second floor of the left wing on the extreme northeast side. One is small and occupies the corner of the building. The other is larger, adjacent to the first, and has windows facing east. This had been Trujillo's office. The smaller room, which had served as his waiting room, was the one I occupied.

I was a prisoner in that office on the night of September 25, 1963. With me were my Vice President, the President of the Senate, and several Ministers. Through the windows, we saw the shadows of the pacing guards, with their machine guns. None of our captors entered the room in which we were being held except the chief of the corps of aides. The rest were in the large room that Trujillo had occupied.

If anyone had arrived that dawn to tell me that Trujillo was there, that he had come back to occupy his office in the National Palace, I would have believed it. That night the Chief had come back in spirit to command his men in arms. Outside, the city was in a state of alarm as police patrols went about raiding houses to arrest anyone who might be influential enough to mobilize the masses, and lifelong Trujilloists congratulated each other on the telephone and ecstatically celebrated the "return" of the departed one.

Social Sectors in the
Armed Forces

The Armed Forces of the Dominican Republic had its own middle class, including all three strata—a middle class produced within and by the Armed Forces through promotions. In Trujillo's last years, and especially after 1947, many youths from the various strata enrolled in military institutes. Ramfis' military retinue, for example, was made up principally of young men from the upper and middle strata of the civilian middle class. The Air Force's top leadership consisted of young men from the lower and middle strata of the civilian middle class. To a lesser extent, the same was true of the Navy. In the infantry— known in our country simply as the Army—and in the police, the forces were predominantly from the lower stratum.

The Armed Forces underwent the same experiences—although on a smaller scale—as the rest of the country. Middle-class youth turned against the moral code and political outlook of their parents. In the very bastions of the all-powerful dictator, in his own Armed Forces, ardent young anti-Trujillo factions were growing. This came about in a peculiar way. These young men believed that the Army ought to be governed by rules and regulations, yet they found it run by personal whims. The dictator and his son Ramfis made anyone a colonel or general if it suited their fancy. Furthermore, these young men believed that the Army should be above the shifts of politics, that it should not be an arena for business, that it should not serve the private interests of anyone. For these young men, the democracy established on February 27, 1963, was a lamentable failure, because it opened no doors to realizing their ideals—at least, not within the Armed Forces.

Their complaint was valid, but this can be explained. When I came to power, the conspiracy to overthrow my government had already begun. In fact, it was so far advanced that a high official thought that it would be prudent for me to talk to the military even before I took office. Had I made even a single change in the military command, my government would have lasted only weeks, perhaps only days.

Both the military and the civilian middle classes were poisoning themselves and the country as a whole with their perpetual gossip and rumors. It was virtually impossible for me to deal with this flood of lies, to analyze them, to try to pinpoint the source, to distinguish the politically motivated slander from that personally motivated.

Both military and civilian middle classes were hustling about for privileges, favors, gifts—anything that they could get for nothing, that would overlook their lack of skill or training. The military was constantly requesting a government-owned holding in the country or one in the city, or permits to bring cars into the country without paying the sizable import duties. They were military men, but they were attempting to engage in business activities that had nothing to do with their military duties.

I realize that these are characteristics of the Armed Forces in any underdeveloped country, and I point them out because an awareness of them may increase understanding of the problems of Latin American countries whose development is at a stage similar to that of the Dominican Republic in 1963. Although I frequently heard rumors to this effect, I never had proof that the U.S. military mission in Santo Domingo conspired to overthrow my democratic government. I am certain that if a captain in the U.S. mission had said that the government should be overthrown, this would have been done within an hour, because a U.S. captain had greater authority over the Dominican military high command than the people, the Constitution, and the President.

Nevertheless, I am also certain that nothing of this sort could have happened in Mexico. All strata of the Mexican military are fervently patriotic; they love their country; they do not feel humiliated or frustrated or embittered being Mexicans, but entirely the opposite. This is in sharp contrast to the Dominican middle class, which with few exceptions has no love of country. And the military middle class, also with few exceptions, shares the attitude of its civilian counterpart. In Chile, military officers do not sustain themselves with rumors or become disturbed by gossip. They feel secure, unthreatened by impending justice, because the Armed Forces are a responsible institution, well liked by the people. The absence of guilt complexes testifies to the fact that they have not abused the people or turned on them the weapons the Republic has entrusted to them. In Uruguay, officers do not go to the President for grants of land, property, or tax exemptions, because they are men well qualified for the positions they hold, sufficiently educated to leave the Army at any time and live by their profession, perhaps better than in the Army. In any case, they know that at the end of their military duty they will receive a pension that will allow them to live out their lives in security. These men become soldiers because they chose military service as their vocation, and not as a way to make a living or an avenue to power.

The Dominican Armed Forces are among the most backward in the Americas, not only because their country is backward but also because their organization itself is backward. It is a way of life and an area of competition mirroring its civilian counterpart—that is, a man joins the service to obtain a good position and to get rich.

The young middle-class men who began forming anti-Trujillo ranks within the Armed Forces at the time the Trujillo family was ousted—many of whom were thrown out of the Army after the September coup—felt the need to transform the military into a stable, specialized organization. They discussed their concept with low-ranking officers, men of the lower stratum of the middle class who had received their last promotion during the Trujillo regime. The ideas voiced in informal meetings and in chats within the camps remained like seeds scattered in the air here and there about the barracks. The seeds were few, to be sure, but a single kernel of corn that is sown in fertile ground at the proper time can produce a number of ears, each bearing thousands of new kernels. In similar fashion, ideas are spread that lead to innovations in social and political processes.

The Dominican people are fertile ground for the seeds of democracy. And the Dominican people are represented in the Armed Forces by soldiers and trainees, and like the lower civilian stratum of the middle class, they remain close to the masses. As long as this sector does not advance toward the middle stratum, it retains this close contact. The military equivalent of the people, alongside the military equivalent of the lower stratum of the middle class—soldiers and trainees alongside lieutenants, captains, even majors—is fertile soil for those seeds, which sooner or later must take root.

Under the democratic regime, the upper stratum and part of the middle stratum in the Armed Forces acted exactly like their civilian counterparts. In the military sector, the coup was effected by only twenty-six generals and colonels, impelled by the same fear and ambition, the same unwillingness to accept social changes, and the same drive for power and material gain as the civilian sector. If the civilian and military masses had been consulted, there would have been no coup. But governments are rarely overthrown to better the lot of the masses; instead, the intended beneficiaries are minorities who constitute the leadership of civilian and military sectors. Thus, it would be foolish to expect that the masses would be consulted. This happens only among democrats, who hold that the legitimate source of power is the will of the majority, and certainly not among plotters, who consider force the key to power.

The lowest social levels, both civilian and military, had no part in the coup. Could the government have been based on these people—the lower stratum of the civilian middle class, the workers, the unemployed? Unfortunately, such a government would have collapsed. Among these people, few were trained sufficiently to handle the mechanics of public administration. But the case of the military was a little different. Among the lieutenants, captains, and majors were men of greater moral and intellectual stature than the colonels and generals. These younger officers belonged to a generation that because of its timing more than anything else, was essentially anti-Trujillo. The colonels and generals were the cream of the intermediate ranks of Trujilloists. They had never murdered for SIM, but they had received the benefits of the dictatorship. The constitutional government could not promote the younger officers to top military rank because of the opposition of the senior officers, who had been infected by fear transmitted by the upper stratum of the civilian middle class in order to assure itself of coming to power by means of a coup. And following that coup, no other government could introduce new elements to the top military echelon, either, without the simultaneous emergence of a reorganization movement within the Armed Forces.

Yet even with a reform, could a stable army be expected to exist in an unstable country? If an army is part of a society that is built on a shaky foundation, must it not necessarily be a shaky element, too?

This may or may not be so. Under Trujillo, the military was stable, solid, the bedrock that supported that structure of crime. Terrorism lent it stability. What can take the place of terrorism? Democratic security, the kind that permits the Army to function as an honest service honorably treated. Under a democratic government, the Dominican military man must cease being a bureaucrat in uniform under the constant threat of discharge should he fail to accede to his superior officer's whim. Instead, he must become a professional soldier subject to rules and regulations. If that change is effected, it may still be possible to establish democracy in the Dominican Republic. However, the time left to democracy in the Americas seems to be exceedingly short and constantly threatened by devastating hurricanes and annihilating thunderbolts.

The high command of the coup seized power on September 25, 1963, and then invited the parties behind the overthrow to form a government. As these parties had greater respect for the representatives of the United States than for the Dominican people, they were intimidated by the vigorous reaction of U.S. Ambassador Martin, who refused to endorse the coup. Wanting no responsibility for the withholding of U.S. backing, the parties behind the over-throw set up a civilian triumvirate to wield the power of the state. These three selected one of their number to be a President. The absence of integrity in the middle class is evidenced by the fact that the President of the triumvirate had been head of the Central Electoral Board and as such had signed the certificates confirming my election. He seemed to think nothing of disavowing his own authority. Middle-class Dominican life is full of examples of self-betrayal. In their profound wisdom, the people called the new regime "the triumviriate," meaning that it was Viriato Fiallo's government, and the very day of the overthrow, they began once again to call Santo Domingo "Ciudad Trujillo," and to shout "Long live the Chief!" to mark in a bitter joke the revival of Trujillo's rites.

As members of the triumvirate proved unsatisfactory to the instigators of the coup, they were replaced by other, more adaptable men. At the end of nine months, none of the original triumvirate remained, and the three members had been reduced to two by the impossibility of finding a successor for the third man.

On the day of the overthrow—in fact, after the first hour —the beatings, imprisonments, and forced entry without warrants began. People were expelled from the country. The police swung into action, and terrorism was rampant in the streets. Offices were raided. Slanderous propaganda in the depraved language of Trujillo reappeared in the press and on the radio. Paid propaganda in foreign newspapers extended the persecution of Dominican exiles to other countries. Inevitably, before the end of the year, this virulent campaign of hatred produced some political assassinations in the Trujillo manner.

The leaders of the 14th of June, convinced that Trujillo's Dominican Republic was the same as Batista's Cuba and that consequently Castro's revolution could be duplicated in Santo Domingo, realized that the new government was a revival of Trujilloism. Still believing that they could repeat in the Dominican Republic that legendary revolution brought off by the youth of the 26th of July in the Cuba of 1957 and 1958, they took to the mountains. But after a few days, guerrillas from various parts of the country came down from the mountains to surrender themselves to the government. They were unarmed and carried improvised white flags—torn shirts tied to the ends of limbs cut from trees—so that from afar it could be seen that they came in peace and submission. They were received with a stream of bullets. Lawyers, doctors, architects, students, and workers were killed, including the 14th of June President, Manuel Tavarez Justo, and several others of its leaders. Three years before, Tavarez Justo's wife and two of her sisters had been beaten to death in a cane field by Trujillo SIM henchmen, while Tavarez Justo and the husband of one of the two sisters were in a prison in a city in the north. What Trujillo had left undone, his heirs had finished.

Tavarez Justo's murder was a legacy from Trujillo. Among the generals and colonels who had taken part in the coup were a few who had impatiently waited two and a half years for an excuse to do away with Tavarez Justo. Something impelled these men to kill the President of the 14th of June, to murder him without a trace of pity. What was it? Were they terrified that Tavarez Justo might know damning things that he could reveal at any moment? What was the cause of this irrational hatred for a man who through his family had been one of Trujilloism's most tragic victims? Or was it precisely the injustice he had endured that was his crime?

Tavarez Justo was loathed by all the UCN leaders. Because the triumvirate was made up of UCN members, the political responsibility for the crime fell on that party's shoulders. And in these days, Fiallo was the object of many attacks and assassination attempts.

Tavarez Justo had been an impassioned, honest leader, driven to constant activity in order to keep his party to a political line far enough to the left to prevent it from falling into the Communist camp. The Catorcita youth openly admired the Fidel Castro who had toppled Batista after a long siege of guerrilla fighting. This made them very vulnerable to Communist penetration. Tavarez Justo had never allowed the Communists to gain control of his party. But after his death, the youth of the middle class, who were mostly Catorcitas (though many later became Revolutionary Social Christians), were left without a leader. It was a confused and dangerous time for the youth. If the democratic government had sullied the youths' image of democracy with thievery, with abuses of its power, with submission to reactionary forces, with undignified international conduct, the youth movement would have reacted to the assassination of Tavarez Justo with a surge toward Communism.

History shows that there is no redemption for countries that murder their nonconforming minorities. Nonconformism is the yeast of progress. To annihilate is not to govern. Only the man who knows how to lead knows how to govern. The fearful man neither can nor will ever learn to lead. Those who fear nonconformist minorities lack the authority and the capacity to be leaders. Fear, the basest instinct, can produce only crime or servility.

The killing of Tavarez Justo and his companions did nothing to calm the military leaders, who were fighting among themselves for financial gain and political power. The Armed Forces became the battleground of various generals-turned-politicians, each resolved to have greater influence than the next on the officers and soldiers, and so to have greater power. Those who operated business ventures, particularly those dealing in contraband of every kind, spread their gains among the officers so as to buy support. They distributed state-owned real estate in the capital among their favorites, and used soldiers and military funds to build houses for themselves. *Listín Diario* published a photograph of soldier bricklayers, each with a gun in his belt, carrying mortar or wielding a level. Corruption grew to such alarming proportions that many foreign newsmen were outraged. Among these were that Pulitzer Prize winner who had devoted seven months of his career to assisting in the overthrow of the constitutional government and had accused CIDES of training thousands of guerrillas. In one of several articles on Dominican affairs that he had written after the overthrow, for the *New York World-Telegram,* he claimed that Dominican generals were dishonoring the revolution. What revolution? Since when has a *coup d'état* been raised to the status of a revolution?

When politicians—bad ones, to be sure—bring military men into the area of politics, they simultaneously bring politics to the barracks. Because soldiers have little understanding of politics, the barracks variety of politics is the worst. Politics is an art and science of constant changes, of ceaseless agitation. But when changes and agitation enter the barracks, they elbow out the classic virtues on which the very existence of the armed forces depends: discipline, the subordinate's respect for his commanding officer, and the commanding officer's respect for the rules. The coup effected by the military had released a poison that was slowly seeping through the Armed Forces. The fact that the poison may take a year or ten years to have an effect is less important to Dominican history than the certainty that these effects will stop.

About the middle of June, 1964, some eight and a half months after the coup, several cities and towns in the

Dominican interior lived through a night of terror comparable only to the blackest nights of the Trujillo regime. Under cover of darkness, groups of soldiers descended on hundreds of houses in which the occupants slept unaware of what was to come. When the doors opened, the soldiers burst into the houses, seized father, son, brother, and dragged them away to the barracks. There were cases in which as many as thirty guards jumped one man, kicking and beating him, breaking arms, legs, ribs, and hitting him in the face with their rifle butts.

What was the reason for this? The head of the triumvirate satisfied the press with the explanation that orders had gone out to take measures to prevent a riot that, according to rumors, the 14th of June was planning to set off on that date. Since the government thought that the Catorcitas were thinking—it decided to take immediate preventive action. By thinking? No, with the toe of a boot, with the butt of a gun, with everything to make those who think badly think better.

A month later, the UCN's former presidential candidate made a surprising statement: The soldiers responsible for those outrages ought to be punished. It was like trying to retrieve spilled water long after it had been poured on dry soil. Or had Fiallo not known, when he encouraged the coup, when he signed the proclamation, when his party established a regime supported by bayonets, that this would be the inevitable outcome of his acts?

The Youth and the Masses—
Reserve of the Future

After the 1963 coup, what forces were left in the Dominican Republic to make a new attempt at democratic organization?

From the political standpoint, there remained only the avowedly popular parties and the middle-class youth movements: the Reform Party, which had been founded during the democratic government's administration; the PRD, my party, which emerged from the coup stronger than it had ever been during the 1962 campaign; the Revolutionary Social Christian party; and the 14th of June, which had been outlawed after the coup.

Practically nothing was left of the social organizations, not even the labor federations. One of these—the favorite of the Inter-American Regional Workers' Organization (Organización Regional Interamericana de Trabajadores, or ORIT) and of the AFL-CIO—had been led by men who openly endorsed the overthrow. The strongest, the Christian labor central, had declared its opposition to the overthrow, through the press, but its only concern had been to obtain higher wages or more benefits for its affiliates. The FOUPSA-CESITRADO (Frente Obrero Unido pro Sindicatos Autónomos–Central Sindical de Trabajadores Dominicanos, or United Labor Front for Autonomous Unions–Central Union of Dominican Workers), the group most active in defending democratic institutions, had too little organization to oppose the coup government. A fourth labor body, called simply the Union (la Unión), was very tiny. In spite of all these drawbacks, Dominican workers had fought harder against the September coup than their Cuban counterparts had against Batista's March, 1952, coup, but their efforts had been too scattered and had lacked over-all organization.

The so-called moving forces of the country—the chambers of commerce, industrial groups, management organizations, and property owners' associations—had financed and supported the overthrow, and thereafter had poured all their efforts into consolidating the new regime. A few voices of protest had been raised in professional circles, but the organizations of professional men had been unable to reach agreement with each other. Months later, a group of lawyers decided to fight the new regime, but by then it was too strong to listen to protests or petitions.

In short, all organizations consisting of people from the middle or upper stratum of the middle class—except for political groups made up exclusively of young people from those social strata—either backed the overthrow or were totally indifferent. Dominican democracy could expect nothing from these organizations. Many of their leaders lost in an hour the prestige that they had accumulated over the course of years. And the only reason for this was that the social groups that they represented were sick. Society was sick from the inside out, and a rotten tree has never been known to bear healthy fruit.

The only hope that democracy might someday be re-

established in the Dominican Republic lay in the country's youth, particularly youngsters around twenty, and in
the great masses—especially the latter. For the youth were
under the influence of Communism, and this influence was
spreading more and more the longer the new dictatorship
remained in power.

When I speak of the youth, I mean the civilian, the
clergy, and the military. And when I speak of the lower
classes, I mean the civilian and the military. Young officers
and priests are not isolated from the people or the times
in which they live. Although the organizations to which
they are committed subject them to special pressures that
cause them to react to events in a particular way, unquestionably they share the concerns of their generation, the
sensitivity of their age, and the desire to be useful that is
innate in the young. As for the masses, either in the barracks or the slums, they still constitute the best reserve of
the Dominican Republic.

The men and women of the people live in a complete
society of their own, and that is why they have structural,
meaningful interrelationships. They are not intrinsically
weak, as are the people of the middle class. Let us observe
a family in the middle stratum of the middle class. The
head of the family must maintain his position and his
family must, therefore, live in a suitable house. His wife
must have clothes in keeping with her position. He must
own more than one suit lest he give an impression of
stinginess that is traditionally bad form. The country's
elite is small, and all its members know each other; in fact,
most of them see each other daily. The furniture in the
house must be proper, and the children must wear shoes.
All of this adds up to anywhere from 100 to 300 pesos a
month more than the man earns—usually he is the only
one in the family who holds a job—and making up the
difference is no easy matter. This family lives in an environ-

ment that it does not belong in. As a unit of society, it is intrinsically weak because it is burdened with obligations that it cannot meet. Though a middle-class family might favor a constitutional democratic regime, at the first hint of a political crisis it will throw its support to the group in which it has relatives, friends, and contacts, even though this group is bent on a coup. To such a family, the only real crisis is the one affecting its daily existence. That crisis it must surmount, even if at the price of betraying its desire for something better for the country. In that social sector, the youngest can have integrity because they do not support themselves, much less maintain families, and because in recent years it has been the fashion for youth the world over to dress less expensively and to gear their lives to fewer social demands.

The head of a poor slum family has none of these middle-class problems. He can live in a hut that, if need be, he fashions himself out of blocks, cardboard, tin plates, and scrap lumber that he collects here and there. Often his wife has only one dress, which was given to her by the mistress of the home in which she worked as a servant. The man wears an old shirt and torn trousers that he or his wife or a neighbor has patched. In the slums, everyone dresses this way, so no one feels inferior among his friends and neighbors. The furniture consists of boxes, an old table, and some rickety chairs that he and his wife found somewhere and repaired and painted. The children run around barefoot and naked. They do not feel ashamed, as all the other children are in the same state. If the mother works in a better-class home or takes in washing or ironing, she provides the food. If the father finds an odd job, he buys rice, bananas, meat. But even if both mother and father are out of work and the family has nothing to eat, the spirit of brotherhood is so alive and strong among the poor that the neighbors will always provide something. These people, even though they have barely enough to sustain themselves, know how to share with a natural graciousness.

The same holds true for the military. Guards—that is, privates—live in the slums. They share their few possessions and their free time with other slum dwellers. They understand their neighbors' circumstances and exchange ideas with them. They are soldiers, and therefore subject to discipline, and in the barracks they perform their duties in the prescribed manner. But they cannot erase the marks left on them by their home lives, which lead them to form attitudes different from those in the Army camps. Eventually their character is molded by both elements in this duality, but as social beings, their reactions as citizens will outweigh their military surroundings.

The people of the slums have an integrity that makes them mentally and psychologically healthier than the middle stratum of the middle class. The latter are not in harmony with themselves because they do not live in the environment in which they belong. They are full of complexes; they are bitter, they are frustrated, they have lost their self-respect. The result is that flood of gossip, slander, and vileness, that abundance of divorce, broken homes, and personal enmities, and that unprincipled personal and social behavior—all of which come as a shock to the foreign visitor who comes to observe Dominican life. Such emotional instability numbs the intelligence with false concepts. If the upper stratum of the middle class has no concept of democracy, it is understandable, because this group does its thinking not with its brains but with its bank accounts. It has no brain cells, only dollars. The middle stratum has no concept of democracy because the innumerable complexes created by its false social values have stifled its intelligence. These people do not think with dollars; they are governed by unbridled passions, resentments, and frustrations.

But the thinking of the masses is clear, sometimes unexpectedly profound. It is not deformed by complexes, because the masses are true to themselves. They hope to better their lot in life, and struggle to do so, but they are not ashamed. When a man is not satisfied with his fate and works to change it, he does not develop complexes because his psychological and intellectual efforts are directed into healthy channels. What makes a human being mentally ill is to have aspirations and not struggle to achieve them, to have wants and not do anything to satisfy them. Although it is not at once apparent, the soul resents being pressured to be evil by the financial necessity to engage in corruption, and later reveals that resentment in internal disharmony.

The Dominican masses are blessed with an intelligence, a natural decency, and a goodness that impress the most critical observer. Until 1961, they had never had an active part in the political scene. Before Trujillo, they had been less numerous and lived mostly in the country. They had been handled by local bosses, who manipulated them according to the dictator's needs. They were cheap labor for his factories and manpower for his army. After Trujillo's death, they were told, for the first time in Dominican history, that they were an important part of the nation and that they had a right to participate in making its history. The PRD did this, in 1961. A year and a half later, the masses set up the first true Dominican democracy, a democracy of social reform.

Throughout the political campaign that made possible the establishment of such a democracy, the masses were told every lie that might confuse them, but they were never deceived. Slander was hurled at them in the hope of deflecting their aspirations, but their innate decency guided them truly. An attempt was made to use them to oppose their own destiny, but their inherent goodness held them to the course they had chosen. Neither coercion nor bribery nor deceptive propaganda deflected them an inch from that course.

The masses played no part in the 1963 overthrow, and at no time did they yield to it. Some days after the coup, the parties behind it planned a demonstration in order to prove to the world that they had the people's support. Committees from five parties went all over the country to recruit men and women for the demonstration. But when the rally was held, there were more policemen than participants—and there were only about 1,000 policemen. A United States newsman estimated that there were fewer than 700 participants. Even more telling was the general strike decreed by the business community some days before the coup. This was intended to be the decisive action that would clearly justify intervention by the military. But popular reaction was so dangerous that the strike lasted only a day. The "Christian demonstrations" had already been a ludicrous failure. And now that the businessmen's strike had also collapsed, the military high command was denied a political recourse on which to depend and had to show its hand openly.

As I have said earlier, a sizable part of the lower-middle class lives in close contact with the masses and in the same conditions. Most of the PRD leaders who had contact with the people came from the lower-middle class. Many of them had workshops, small businesses, or occupations of various sorts. They had come to party headquarters or to my home, saying that they knew nothing about politics but that they liked the party and wanted to work for it. When they spoke, I was impressed by the clarity of their ideas, the originality of their arguments, the boldness of many of their plans, always decent, always aboveboard. I was impressed by the depth of their feelings about the Dominican tragedy. I do not remember a single conversation with any of these men and women that was not conducted on a high level—with a total absence of gossipmongering. Later, in the last two weeks of the campaign, when the UCN resorted to violence against the PRD—armed riots, crosses of red paint to obliterate the letters of our emblem—and personal attacks on Miolán and myself, those in the lower-middle class who were not already members of the PRD, flocked to join. Their response to the ignoble was an act of justice, as was that of the masses. Even a part, though not the majority, of the middle stratum—it must be acknowledged—decided to cast its fate with ours. Among these people, Father Láutico García's accusation, because it contained injustices, produced some favorable reaction for the PRD.

During a meeting at party headquarters one day around the middle of 1962, a man dressed in work clothes got to his feet and began to speak. His language was beautiful, almost Biblical. In the most vigorous phrases, he recalled all that I had been saying on the radio for the past months. I asked him what he did, and he said that he owned a small shoemaker's shop. Men like him began joining our ranks by the thousands, and they learned with incredible alacrity. Men and women who had reached the age of twenty, twenty-five, or even thirty, without ever hearing a word about social, economic, or political problems, within a few months created for themselves a whole world of concepts, expressed in passionate, deeply felt terms. It was obvious that for years and years they had carried in their souls the desire to hear such concepts and to be able to communicate them. Their ideas were of the common good, of social justice, of liberty; they were concerned with reasons, feelings, and concepts that would benefit many, not themselves alone. If they had spent their lives thinking only of their personal or family problems, of how to solve them and without caring whether others solved their problems, these people could not have grasped so quickly, and with such clarity and accuracy, the message that the PRD brought to them.

The 1962 elections were the first demonstration that the masses and the majority of the lower-middle class had received that message and were ready to make the transition from passive spectators to onstage actors in their country's drama. The vote in favor of the PRD had been overwhelming. On election day, the masses and the lower middle class—particularly the poor in this stratum—began lining up at the polls at four in the morning in many places, and before five in most places. The second demonstration of the new attitude of the masses and the majority of the lower stratum occurred some months after the PRD administration was overthrown, at the beginning of May, 1964.

In those days, uprisings in the capital's slums took place on any pretext. Taxi drivers had decided to strike, and news that the police had orders to arrest the organizers forced the advancement of the strike schedule. On Saturday at two o'clock in the afternoon, slum dwellers, in an outburst of anger, staged an uprising the likes of which had never been seen before. Men, women, and children ran through the city stoning cars, breaking windows, blocking traffic, tossing garbage, and burning wood, old tires, anything combustible. Businesses in the smart section of the city were forced to close down. For several days, actual warfare raged between the people and the police, and though the Dominican Republic has a higher ratio of police to population than any other country in the world— 17,000 police to a population of about 3.5 million—the riot could not be quelled until the coup government called out literally thousands of soldiers.

Nothing of the kind had happened in the history of the Republic. The uprisings against Ramfis and his uncles had never reached the slums, but had pitted the middle and upper strata of the middle class against Ramfis' forces. Nonetheless, the May, 1964, uprising was classed by the elite—and by the government, of course—as an abortive strike. But it was not a strike. It was an explosion of popular rage, and any intelligent observer could predict more and bigger explosions to come. There was unquestionably a link between the awakening of the political consciousness of the masses, manifested in the 1962 elections, and the violence that erupted in May, 1964. The street fighting was not the outcome of the taxi drivers' strike. It was a typical political uprising to protest a political order detested by the people. The taxi drivers' strike merely triggered it.

To the rulers of the Dominican Republic, the masses are trash, plebeian trash; the mob. If the masses protest or rebel, the government simply orders out fire hoses, machine guns, or blackjacks. The men running the country have no respect for the masses' votes, because they regard them as votes without quality; they do not give consideration to plebeian protests, because they do not recognize their right to protest. They do not regard them as Dominicans or even as men and women who have been brought into the world with certain rights. The government groups belong to the upper and middle strata of the middle class, and they feel that only people of their social scale are entitled to demand, protest, or require that they be heard.

The style of government established after the coup was the direct opposite of the constitutional government, which had set about reorganizing public finances and the national economy on the principle that wealth should be distributed so that the great masses would participate in creating it and therefore in its distribution. The new government had proceeded to do just the opposite. It disorganized public funds by placing them in a few privileged hands, thereby diluting the creation of wealth and blocking its distribution to the masses. Nine months after the overthrow, a few hundred families of the middle and upper strata of the middle class enjoyed greater wealth than ever before; meanwhile, thousands upon thousands of workers were jobless, small businesses were shuttered, and peasant farmers migrated to the cities.

In this kind of political economy, the misery of the masses deepened, but their demands were answered only with police terror. More and more, with their newly awakened consciousness, the masses became convinced that the only way out was to fight for a better life.

Ten months after the 1963 coup, a growing hunger among the masses aggravated the plight of the lower-middle class—first the poor members and then those with greater resources. And the day will also come when an important part of the middle stratum will become convinced that there are not enough privileges to go around for all the families of their class. When that day comes, the hands on the reins of power will begin to tremble.

There remain, then, people prepared to build democracy in the Dominican Republic. But before attempting once again to erect the house of freedom and justice, these people will look to their past, they will look to the Americas, and ask: "Is it worth it to start building again only to have everything taken away from us? Russia is helping Cuba, but who will help us?" The question demands a clear answer.

The problem facing the Dominicans is not whether they can build another democracy, but whether there is still time enough for this task in a Latin American country crushed by the ills of centuries.

The crisis of democracy in the Dominican Republic is the crisis of democracy in the Americas. It has its special Dominican aspects, but it is not exclusively Dominican. When the government elected by the Dominican people on December 20, 1962, was toppled, a dagger was thrust into Dominican flesh, and its point pierced the heart of America. America is many and yet it is one. Everything that has happened in one American country has happened in others. At least, this is the lesson that history has taught, and history is not only a tale told of the past, but also, and above all, a mirror of what is yet to come.

Index